Valued Voices

An Interdisciplinary Approach to Teaching and Learning

Deborah A. Wooten
Glenwood Landing Elementary School
North Shore Central School District
Sea Cliff, New York, USA

INTERNATIONAL
**Reading
Association**

International Reading Association
800 Barksdale Road, PO Box 8139
Newark, Delaware 19714-8139, USA

www.reading.org

The International Reading Association attempts, through its publications, to provide a forum for a wide spectrum of opinions on reading. This policy permits divergent viewpoints without implying the endorsement of the Association.

Director of Publications   Joan M. Irwin
Editor in Chief, Books   Matthew W. Baker
Permissions Editor   Janet S. Parrack
Associate Editor   Tori Mello
Publications Coordinator   Beth Doughty
Association Editor   David K. Roberts
Production Department Manager   Iona Sauscermen
Art Director   Boni Nash
Senior Electronic Publishing Specialist   Anette Schütz-Ruff
Electronic Publishing Specialist   Cheryl J. Strum
Electronic Publishing Assistant   Jeanine K. McGann

Project Editor   Christian A. Kempers

Cover   Connelly Design

Library of Congress Cataloging in Publication Data
   Valued Voices: an interdisciplinary approach to teaching and learning/Deborah A. Wooten.
      p.   cm.
   Includes bibliographical references (p.) and index.
ISBN 0-87207-270-3
   1. Language arts (Elementary).   2. Interdisciplinary approach in education.   3. Children—Books and reading.   I. Title.
LB1576.W665   2000   00-026946
372.6'044—dc21

For Bee, Gene, Katie, and Matt

Contents

Foreword

I have known hundreds of talented teachers during my years as professor of early childhood, elementary education, reading education, and children's literature, but I seldom find one who combines the unique talents of Deborah Wooten. She is one of the most gifted teachers I have ever seen.

Deborah Wooten is a practitioner in metacognition. She expects students to think about their thinking and she structures ways for them to reflect on the work they do. She shows by example how readers and writers move to higher level thinking skills. Using a technique of having students make connections to a book she reads aloud, Deborah conducts a symphony of reading, writing, listening, speaking, and thinking skills. Her strategies require that students create, describe, and categorize the type of connections they make. I have observed her students probe deeply into layers of meaning as they discuss their responses to text.

Deborah Wooten is a dedicated teacher. She is a member of professional organizations, reads their journals, attends and presents at educational conferences, and keeps up with research in the field. She knows why she does what she does in the classroom. She is knowledgeable about the theories of how children learn language. She implements classroom practices that are supported by research. She sees what works best for her students on an individual basis, and knows why it works. In addition, Deborah prepares her students to meet local, state, and national standards while integrating ongoing assessment of their performance.

Deborah Wooten is a lifelong learner. She is continually on the lookout for new ideas, new materials, and new books. She is constantly trying to improve her own teaching. When she finds a new book that will enrich her curriculum, she can hardly wait to get it into her classroom. Like many teachers, Deborah often spends her own money on books for her classroom.

Valued Voices: An Interdisciplinary Approach to Teaching and Learning was developed directly from a talented teacher's classroom. When you read this book you will gain new insights about teaching. You will be amazed at how this interdisciplinary approach blends theory, practice, and research so successfully.

Bernice E. Cullinan
New York University
New York, New York, USA

Acknowledgments

I am humbled when I think of all the people who helped with the writing of this book. The students' voices inspired me to write, while my husband Gene and two children Katie and Matt, friends, and faith in God motivated me to sit at the computer working for countless hours. I also appreciate all the support, love, and understanding shown to me by my friends, the members of our writer's group: Bee Cullinan, Ginnie Schroder, Marilyn Scala, Joie Hinden, and Ann Lovett. I am truly grateful to Joan Irwin for opening the door for publishing this book and to Bee Cullinan for being a role model for me professionally and personally. In addition I deeply appreciate Chris Kempers and Matt Baker for working diligently shaping and editing this book. It was an honor to work with the students who provided me with the voices to share in this book. I thank Andrew and Brian Stern who inspired me and still do. I also thank Kelly Alverson, Taylor Bodo, Joey Bouganim, Danny Carleton, Peter Coleman, Taylor Crane, Michael Curtis, Bobby Gallagher, Michael Gentile, Caitlin Goetz, Adam Greenberg, Kelly Henry, Doug Harrigan, Victoria La Rosa, Kaitlyn LeBlang, Robert Lynn, James Micucci, Todd Migden, Thomas Miller, Nicole Minkoff, David Muller, Sarah Papisdero, Dawn Qadir, David Radford, Raysana, Kerry Rigley, Hiroe Sakamoto, Scott Savinetti, Erin Schreiner, Liza Schreiner, Chandni Singh, Serik Slobodskoy, Chelsea Spallone, Katie Uihlein, Andrew Worrell.

Introduction

I am writing this on the last day of school—a half day for my fifth graders. I have just enough time to do my end-of-the-year awards ceremony, sign yearbooks, do one last read-aloud, and hand out report cards. Good-byes have all been said, and the children have disappeared into a summer of the beach and water park before their fall entry into middle school.

Sure, I'd like to be out playing too. But my principal has decided he wants to group all fifth-grade classes into the same area of the building. So I have to stay behind to pack and move my classroom.

So why, in the midst of emptying file cabinets and boxing my large collection of children's literature, am I taking the time to write the introduction for this book? I was inspired by one of my students who handed me a letter just before he left today. He wrote it last night and, with his permission, I want to share it with you in Figure 1 on the next page.

Is there any question that Andrew is expressing in his letter some of his innermost feelings about the transition to middle school? And in expressing those feelings, he has connected them to our class studies of the Civil War and Jefferson Davis (Krynock & Robb, 1999). No, Andrew was not in the gifted program. In fact, at the beginning of the school year he disliked writing so much that he did anything he could to avoid it. He viewed writing as a laborious act of handwriting and answering questions that teachers posed (Graves, 1991). Look at the chaos in one of his writing samples from the beginning of the year, shown in Figure 2 on page 3.

It is difficult to believe that the two pieces in Figures 1 and 2 were written by the same student. Yet transition as dramatic as this is not unusual in my classroom, thanks, I believe, to a teaching methodology I have been researching and developing: a process that gives every child from special education to gifted an equal voice in the community of learners; a process that allows the teacher significant insight into what students know and how they construct their learning (Brooks & Brooks, 1999); one that allows the teacher to discover the ideas conveyed within students' writing despite grammar and style (Shaughnessy, 1977); a process that truly opens the door to divergent thinking and lets each child's genius emerge. My students this year named the methodology *Writing and Sharing Connections*.

Figure 1 Andrew's Letter

Dear Dr. Wooten,

Even though I'm the one leaving GWL, I feel as if it's you. I feel like a small fish entering the huge Atlantic. I feel confused and feel as if troubled waters are coming my way. I will miss GWL. I will miss you. I will treasure everything that you taught me. You have prepared me well for the Middle School. I just wanted to write about why you said that Zachary Taylor is your favorite president. Taylor's daughter eloped with Jefferson Davis. On the honeymoon the newlyweds got sick and Taylor's daughter died. Davis was sick for ten years. The South was in disagreement with the North about freeing slaves. The South broke away from America and elected Davis as president. After the Civil War the North tied up railroad tracks and they called them Jefferson Davis knots. After the war the South hated him and so did the North. He was called the man without his country.

I too will be without a country for a short while. When I enter the Middle School, I will explore, and will hopefully settle into a new country.

Love,
Andrew L Stern

Figure 2   Andrew's Early Fifth-Grade Writing Sample

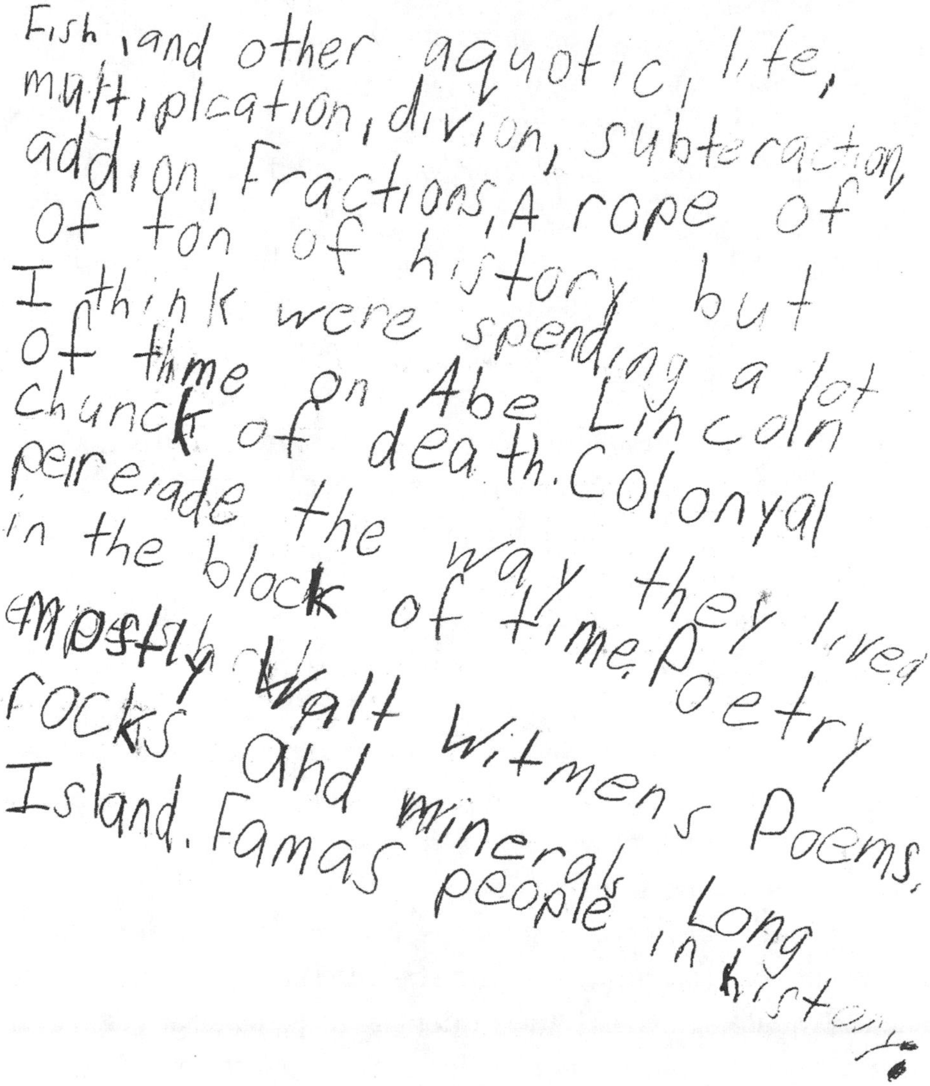

Fish, and other aquotic, life, multiplcation, divion, subteraction, addion, Fractions, A rope of of ton of history but I think were spending a lot of thme on Abe Lincoln chunck of death. Colonyal peirerade the way they lived in the block of time. Poetry mostly Walt Witmens Poems, rocks and minerals Long Island. Famas people in history.

This is a theory-into-practice handbook for teachers who derive satisfaction from their profession but who know there is always a better, more effective way to reach students. The book describes a way to hear all students' voices, to view students as individuals, to assess and learn from students, to promote content-related literature, and to encourage creative and divergent thinking. I have used Writing and Sharing Connections effectively with students in grades 3 through 5.

How Writing and Sharing Connections Began

Writing and Sharing Connections started one morning during a read-aloud session held in a carpeted area of my classroom. I had just read *Nettie's Trip South* by Ann Turner to the class. Normally we would have gone to our desks and responded in our reader's workshop notebooks (Galda, Cullinan, & Strickland, 1997). Later I would call the students back to the carpeted area and ask for volunteers to share their responses with the class. The same few students would probably volunteer, I would tenderly coax a couple of the timid ones to share as well, and we would finish the exercise with many unheard voices. But not today!

Have you ever noticed how enticing a pad of sticky notes can be (commonly referred to as the 3M Company's brand name, "Post-its")? Who would have guessed that ordinary pieces of paper with a strip of adhesive on the back could cause students to write, draw, and jot so freely? Sticky notes are so handy, convenient, and fun that each morning I would put a fresh pad on my desk, and by the closing bell they would be gone. Realizing the magic of these sticky notes, I passed them out to students after reading aloud *Nettie's Trip South*, instructing them to write their feelings about the book. I allowed the students to have discussions at their desks for a few minutes before they wrote their responses. I told them that we *all* would share and display our responses. Then I spent a few minutes interacting with and observing my students. After everyone had written responses, I called each student forward to share what he or she had written. One by one I stuck their notes to a large tablet and labeled each with the student's name. I was amazed at the diversity of responses and the rich discussion that followed. Everyone's work was now displayed with equal prominence. I was particularly impressed with what I learned about my students and how this information could inform my teaching.

As I watched the chart of responses take shape, I realized that we had a document that was a valuable assessment tool. I had a writing sample from each student—an early indication of creativity, mechanics, and comprehension and a few discernible hints about each student's stage of writing development. I also was happy to have heard the voice of every student, instead of just a few volunteers.

The Organization of This Book

I am writing this book because quality interdisciplinary, literature-based methodology for the upper elementary grades has been slow to develop and usually complicated to implement (Galda, Cullinan, & Strickland, 1997). I believe that the methodology I have been using in my classroom motivates students to read and write and to learn across the curriculum. In Chapter 1 you will find a complete overview of how the Writing and Sharing Connections process works and the theory that supports each step in practice. The process is simple to implement, and you do not need many extra supplies. Also in Chapter 1 I talk about the most important foundational element for Connections: the atmosphere in the classroom that allows community to develop.

In Chapter 2, I further explain two essential components of my methodology—graphing and categorizing connections and writing a metacognitive piece. This step in the Connections process provides the teacher with insight on students' thinking and learning.

In truth, however, I cannot write this handbook as well as my students can. So, in Chapter 3 you will visit my classroom at the beginning of the school year as Connections is introduced to a new group of students. I also explain how Writing and Sharing Connections fits into our school day and school year.

Because assessment and learning goals are a major concern, I describe in Chapter 4 how and why many of the U.S. state and national learning goals are satisfied with the Writing and Sharing Connections process. Also included is an explanation of the rubric I use to assess students' writing.

At the beginning of these chapters, I have included a student's metacognitive piece of writing. As I look back on how far these students progressed in one year as writers, readers, thinkers, and presenters, I am still amazed. And I think you will be too.

In Chapters 5 through 7, I show you the work of three specific students throughout a school year. You will read the connections they generated during the school year, along with my analysis of each one. I introduce each book that we write and share connections with, and I highlight a few of my favorite teaching ideas that bridge subject areas and motivate student learning. Also included are the students' three metacognitive pieces written during the year. Throughout these chapters I have noted with each student's connection the different learning goals that it satisfies. To further clarify the U.S. state and national learning goals with regards to each student's connection, I have graphed them to include in the Appendixes.

Throughout Chapters 5, 6, and 7 you will see how the three students I tracked developed as thinkers and writers, how they learned from hearing other students present their writing aloud, and how they naturally crossed the boundaries of subject areas in writing connections.

Chapter 8 introduces diversity and how it is strengthened with Writing and Sharing Connections. This look at diversity includes special education, bilingual, and gifted or accelerated students.

In the Conclusion I try to answer frequently asked questions about my methodology. My goal is to explain the Writing and Sharing Connections process simply and clearly so that teachers can implement it in their classrooms to help students further develop as learners.

I close this Introduction with a metacognitive piece that captures the essences of Writing and Sharing Connections (shown in Figure 3).

Figure 3 Kaitlyn's Metacognitive Piece

Connections   *Kaitlyn LeBlang*

My favorite part of the day is when we write and share connections. I believe writing connections opens up my mind to new ideas about a book we read in the classroom. Connections can be in the form of skits that are funny, sad, or happy. They can also be a piece of poetry I have written. Just about everything has a connection to it! That is what I like about connections. No matter what you put down on that post-it it is always your thoughts and nothing can be wrong. I think that by writing and sharing connections we learn more about how we think.

Chapter 1

Writing and Sharing Connections: An Overview

My thinking has changed through connections by stretching the thought and looking deeper and stronger than ever before. Things are more clear though connections; you can see things differently. My writing gets stronger and more insightful through every word of my connections, and I can see that a tree is more than wood and leaves. A tree is a living organ and a symbol of life and enrichment. A connection could be a tree because a connection grows with you as you write one word after another constructs a connection. A tree grows with every drop of water like every drop of a caring thought.

Andrew

I am a children's bookaholic. I admit it. I buy a lot of children's literature. And there has never been a better time to have a book fetish. There are more than 100,875 children's books in print (Cullinan & Galda, 1998) from which to select the perfect read-aloud experience for my students. I believe the quality of children's literature is at an all-time high. Excellent children's books are available today on a variety of levels that strengthen and inform with history, science, math, art, music, and every subject area. Much of today's literature does more than merely inform (McMahon & Raphael, 1997). The best books lure children into the content and stimulate their brains with new knowledge, while the children are completely distracted by the fun they are having. That's the kind of book I am always looking for: the perfect book for a Writing and Sharing Connections session.

The Materials

Other than literature, you will need only a few additional supplies to prepare for a Connections session.

1. Sticky notes. These notes come in pads and in various sizes and colors. I start with the 3" × 3" size, and at the beginning of the first session I give each child two or three sheets on which to write their connections. Sticky notes are not too expensive, and I have had no problem getting parents to buy them for their children. In fact, after the first few Connections sessions, my students usually start bringing in sticky notes that are dye cut in various designs and printed in amazing color schemes. Writing and Sharing Connections really opens up the creative process in students and outrageous writing materials are just an early indication of that.

2. A 24" × 32" chart tablet. You will need a chart tablet to post children's notes when they finish writing their connections. My school provides these tablets to the teachers. You can find them at school supply stores and at some office supply stores.

3. An easel. You will need an easel to support the chart tablet for all the students to see. I have always been able to find one collecting dust somewhere in my school. If easels are not available in your school, they can be purchased from school supply stores and art supply stores.

4. 8½" × 11" sheets of graph paper. I use graph paper to have students graph all the categories in which they have written connections. How the paper is ruled depends on the grade level of the students and what they are comfortable with. I use ¼" ruling for upper elementary students.

5. A multicolor assortment of markers and a spool of tape. I write the category of the students' connections on the chart tablet with markers. I use the tape to reinforce the sticky note adhesive when attaching it to the chart tablet.

6. A notebook or composition book for each student. I have students use their writer's notebooks for note taking. Some teachers might want students to use their language arts or literature notebook.

Next, I outline step-by-step the Writing and Sharing Connections process and discuss the theory that undergirds this methodology. Within this chapter, and throughout the book, I also talk about the importance of creating a community atmosphere that helps students feel uninhibited about expressing themselves while writing connections or doing any other creative project in your classroom.

The Basic Steps

Following is a brief overview of the steps in the Writing and Sharing Connections process:

Step 1   Move the students to a comfortable location such as a carpeted area of the classroom.

Step 2   Introduce a book to be read aloud. Write the name of the book and the date at the top of a blank chart tablet page (supported by an easel for all to see).

Step 3   Read the book aloud.

Step 4   Have students return to their desks.

Step 5   Allow students time to write their connections to the book on sticky notes.

Step 6   One by one, have students come to the easel and share their connection aloud.

Step 7   Have the class decide on a category in which to classify each connection. Stick each connection to the chart tablet page and write the category and student's name beside it.

Step 8   Have students record the read-aloud book title, date, and everyone's name and category of their connection in their notebooks while others are sharing their connections.

Step 9   Three times each year, graph connections and have students write a metacognitive piece.

Now, let's fill in some of the details of the process and explain the theory on which it is based.

Step 1 Move the students to a comfortable location.

Writing and Sharing Connections must be done in a classroom community that is rich with feelings of togetherness and equality (Peterson, 1992). I have a piece of carpet, approximately 8' × 12', on the floor in the back of my classroom. The carpeted area is a safe haven—a no-stress, no-pressure area of the classroom where everyone can feel totally secure (Johns & Lenski, 1997). Sitting at our desks is the "down-to-business" setting of the classroom, where pencils come out, notes are taken, and students are likely to be working individually, whereas the carpet setting

9

is the "get-away-from-the-grind" setting. Almost all activity on the carpet is done as a group, although because the atmosphere is so relaxed, students don't always realize they are actually working. When we move to the carpet, there is no assigned, organized seating arrangement. Early in the school year students sit beside their friends. Later, as we get to know one another better, I urge them to sit beside someone they have never sat with before.

Step 2 Introduce a book to be read aloud.

I introduce the book purely to stimulate interest and set the mood. Because I always elect to read aloud books that I am enthusiastic about, enticing curiosity about the story is usually easy. Sometimes I have students engage in a "literature talk out," or a literacy conversation prior to the read-aloud experience (Hennings, 1992). Discussions are key to learning (Genishi, McCarrier, & Nussbaum, 1988; Shuy, 1987). I write the name of the book and the date at the top of a blank chart tablet page. Then, I state the title, show the cover artwork, and ask the group what they think the book will be about. I usually offer an interesting piece of knowledge that I obtained from the book, which usually grabs students' attention and catapults us to page one of the book.

Whenever possible, I use a visual aid to help market the book to the students. For example, I put a potato in the center of the carpet and introduced a book about President John F. Kennedy. Imagine the curiosity and the theorizing that occurred as students tried to relate a potato to a president. The book I read aloud gave them the answer: The Joseph Kennedy family moved to the United States because of the potato famine in Ireland in 1845 and 1846. Besides enticing curiosity, the Irish potato added some reality to our history lesson. The students enjoy getting involved in book artifacts. One day I mentioned to my class that we would be reading a book about World War II the following day. The next morning, one student surprised me with his grandfather's World War II Purple Heart, the medal given to soldiers wounded in battle.

Here are a few other tips for introducing a book:

■ Relate the book to something previously discussed or presented in the classroom. For example, "Remember the other day when we were talking about Pirates? I found a book about pirates...."

■ Because the literature I select is almost always content related, I tie the book directly into what we are studying.

Step 3 Read the book aloud.

Much has been demonstrated about the value of reading aloud to students. A tremendous amount of research has been conducted on the subject. The following statements from *Becoming a Nation of Readers* (Anderson, Hiebert, Scott, & Wilkerson, 1985) best illustrate the power of reading aloud:

> The single most important activity for building the knowledge required for eventual success in reading is reading aloud to children. (p. 23)
>
> There is no substitute for a teacher who reads children good stories. It whets the appetite of children for reading and provides a model of skillful oral reading. It is a practice that should continue throughout the grades. (p. 51)

Because reading aloud has been a substantial part of my teaching technique for years, I am quite sure of its numerous benefits. Reading aloud promotes language development and vocabulary and enriches discussion. It promotes intertextual links—links from one piece of literature to another. Further, reading aloud increases students' general knowledge base so that when they encounter new texts, they have knowledge from which to draw in order to comprehend the texts (Steffensen, Joag-Dev, & Anderson, 1979). There is also something about revealing the magic of a good story to a reluctant reader that can motivate the desire to read. And when we gather on the carpet, reading aloud promotes our community atmosphere by uniting us in one focus.

Another benefit of reading aloud is the fortification of listening skills. Hennings (1992) describes listening and reading in the following way:

> Good listeners also are makers of ideas. Listening involves the reception and processing of incoming data. To listen is not just to hear; it is the active construction of meaning from all the signals—verbal and nonverbal—a speaker is sending. In this way, listening is closely akin to reading. (p. 3)

Cullinan and Galda in *Literature and the Child* (1998, p. 51) suggest these tips for reading aloud:

1. Read the book ahead of time, and be familiar with it.
2. Give a brief description of the book or character to establish a context for the listeners.
3. Prune lengthy passages of description, if necessary, to keep interest high.
4. Begin reading aloud slowly; quicken the pace as listeners enter the story world.
5. Look up from the book frequently to maintain eye contact.
6. Interpret dialogue meaningfully.
7. Read the entire book, if possible, or a chapter or more per day to sustain meaning.

Step 4 Have students return to their desks.

There are two reasons for moving the children from the carpet to their desks:

1. The next step in the Connections process is writing, and it is physically easier to write while sitting at a desk.
2. Sitting on the carpet can become uncomfortable after a while. Because we are about to enter the next phase in the Writing and Sharing Connections process, it's a good idea for everyone to be as comfortable as possible.

Step 5 Allow students time to write their connections to the book on sticky notes.

A connection is a personal response to or a transaction with the book read aloud. Each student's connection is personal because every connection is a result of fusing a student's intellect and emotional make-up to their background knowledge (Rosenblatt, 1938/1983; 1978).

At the beginning of the school year I usually find that some students already have had experience responding to literature, usually in response journals. Other students have had no such experience, especially with content-related literature. To be honest, most students who enter my classroom after one or more years of skill-based instruction are uncomfortable with the idea of being allowed and even encouraged to write what they think and feel. These are usually students who have written primarily about topics created and dictated by teachers, typically in well-intentioned but noncontextualized write-a-paragraph drills. So it is not surprising that I see blank stares when we sit at our desks to write our first connections. Suggestions, idea starters, much encouragement, and even some modeling are necessary to get everyone started. Some of the things I do to encourage students to write include the following:

- Model a connection: "The story I just read reminds me of...."
- Share students' connections from previous years. I usually share what I consider a benchmark-level connection and then an exemplar. I find that showing students these exemplars tends to keep them aiming higher and progressing faster in their writing. If you are going to try Writing and Sharing Connections in your classroom, you might use some of the connections in this book as examples.
- Give students an opportunity to chat informally with one another before they start writing. This opens an opportunity for brainstorming ideas. An observation made by one student frequently will trigger a different thought or connection for another student.

Writing and Sharing Connections puts *schema theory* into action. Meaningful learning occurs when one's cognitive structures properly coincide with the material to be learned (Thelen, 1986). Stated more simply, when we read a book aloud, we expect that some bit of information, dialogue, plot, or illustration will remind a student of something he or she already knows. Schema theory suggests that the student will remember and file that new bit of information as learned knowledge more readily by associating it with information that is already accepted in his or her mental filing cabinet, or knowledge base. Writing that connection serves to strengthen the association of the two bits of knowledge and reinforce learning.

Writing and Sharing Connections also allows me a glimpse of a student's background knowledge. Done repeatedly throughout the school year, the Connections process can reveal a great deal about the information stored in those young minds. It provides valuable information that helps me shape my lessons so that learning gaps are addressed, misinformation is repaired, and students' interests are revealed. How many times have I heard teachers wish aloud that they could find the "hot but-ton" that would awaken a certain student's desire to learn? If you are a careful observer, Writing and Sharing Connections can reveal "hot but-tons" in each child.

The five steps covered so far demonstrate no new insight or tech-nique. Teachers have been reading aloud and students have been writing responses to literature for some time (although not necessarily on sticky notes). But beginning with Step 6, the uniqueness of the Writing and Shar-ing Connections process is evident. You are about to see how students can learn from one another as a community, organize their learning ac-cording to schema theory, and think about their thinking (metacognition).

Step 6 One by one, have students come to the easel and share their connection aloud.

It seems that the same handful of bold students who always want to speak out in class discussions get the most attention. Try as we may, there are always a few students who are too timid to voluntarily speak up and be heard. With the one or two most shy students, to call on them turns them red with embarrassment. Yet we all miss important learning op-portunities when we do not get to hear from every student.

The Connections process is a vehicle for hearing every child's voice and viewpoint. Remember that when a connection is written, a student reveals a bit of information he or she already knows, and connects that in-formation to the read-aloud text. When we share our connections aloud, each student presents a learning opportunity for every other student. The class becomes a learning community in the truest sense.

The question is, How do we get *everyone*, even the most timid, to stand in front of the class and share? The answer lies in the classroom en-vironment. My classroom is a safe harbor for learners. One of the rea-sons we write connections on 3" × 3" sticky notes is that they are small and nonthreatening. Most any student, from gifted to learning disabled, can string together enough words to fill a small sticky note. However, if writing that first connection is too difficult for a child, I let him or her create a "response drawing" about the book on the sticky note. (Experi-ence shows that once students hear the connections written by their classmates, they start emulating them. It never takes long for them to find their own voice and begin writing meaningful connections.) When I call on a student to share, he or she stands beside me. There is no harsh judgment to be faced when sharing a connection. Early in the year I establish one rule with the class: We *never* laugh at students when they share a connection.

Connections also are never graded. The sticky note is a safe place for a student to write a "burst of thought" or radiant thinking (Buzan, 1996, p. 57) about the literature that was read aloud. In fact, because connections are an expression of personal point of view, there is never a wrong answer. I always find a positive comment to make after each connection is shared. Even the most crudely written connections with shallow content (especially those from the first two or three Connections sessions of the year) draw some praise about vocabulary employed, content, clear speech, courage, or neat penmanship.

Do the students really respond to this positive atmosphere and reinforcement? I regularly ask my students to give me feedback about how we do things in class. The following comments from Brook are fairly typical of the feedback I receive:

> I get excited when we write and share connections because Dr. Wooten always stands next to me. She also always says something nice to every single person who has a connections. This makes me feel comfortable. So, when I go up to share my connections, I will do a good job. I can't wait for Dr. Wooten to read another book so I can write and share another fabulous connection.

Brook was a very shy student who rarely said anything in class no matter how often I called on her. But after she participated in the Connections process for a few months, notice how eager she became to share with the class. Children are inclined to participate if they feel secure and valued versus being judged. In Brook's case, she felt so accepted, she couldn't wait to share another connection.

Step 7 Have the class decide on a category in which to classify each connection.

Categorizing connections is simple, but also very important in the learning process. Categorizing a connection, or deciding its main idea, is a process by which a student (along with classmates' participation if elicited) revisits his or her response about the book so it can be organized for future retrieval. This adds more *value* to the student's response. Categorizing coincides with the manner in which our minds file and organize information according to schema and the constructivist theories. Let's try a simple exercise:

Just for a moment, think about cars. Chances are your mind went much further than simply thinking about the word *car*. You may have drawn a mental picture of the new car you just bought or want to buy, thought of the make and model of a car that has impressed you in some way, or relived a car accident you experienced and even cringed about the repair bill. In this exercise you have opened your mental file cabinet, found the "car" folder, opened it, and recalled some of the knowledge filed inside.

When we categorize connections, we are helping each child in the room file the knowledge in that connection into their mental file cabinet. We are providing the file folder (the category) if it does not already exist and helping each student place a file of knowledge (the connection) inside. Each child's fund of knowledge also is expanding by listening to peer explanations.

After a student reads aloud his or her connection, I ask all the students, "What category shall we put this connection into?" The category is simply the main idea or theme of the connection. For example, suppose a student writes this connection to a book:

This book reminds me of the movie *The Sound of Music* because the story happens during World War II, just like in the movie.

We would categorize this as a movie connection.

Early in the year, the categories usually include television shows, movies, illustrations, personal experiences, feelings, family, famous people, and so forth. Later in the year, as students learn to search deeper into their knowledge base, the categories will reflect this depth: science, history, point of view, literature, politics, environment, and so on. Remember, there is no set list of categories, but a category for each connection usually will be obvious. In Chapter 3 I will categorize a number of connections to help you get started.

After each student shares a connection we stick the written note to the chart tablet paper and indicate its category. I keep a large assortment of colored marker pens and use a different color for each category. For the connection example explained earlier, I would pick a colored marker, write the word *movie* at the top left of the chart, and stick the student's written connection under the category heading. Then I would write the name (usually just first name) of the student beside or on the sticky note in the same color as the category. If the next connection belongs in a different category, I would use a different color marker pen. (Refer to Figure 4 for a photo of a connection chart.)

One special education student shared her description of categorizing connections:

> I like writing connections. It is a way to write down how you connect to the book you have just read. Dr. Wooten puts our connections on the chart and we categorize them. A couple of examples, of categorizes are feelings and point of view. I like the books we read. We read a lot of great books and connect to them too!!

When students categorize their connections they are revisiting their thinking about what they have heard read aloud and pinpointing the main idea. When students listen to their classmates categorize their connections, they again are revisiting the story read aloud and relating the category to the connection. All students who are actively engaged in this activity critically and creatively construct their learning while monitoring their understanding of the story read aloud (Hennings, 1992; Perkins, 1999).

Figure 4 A Sample Connections Chart

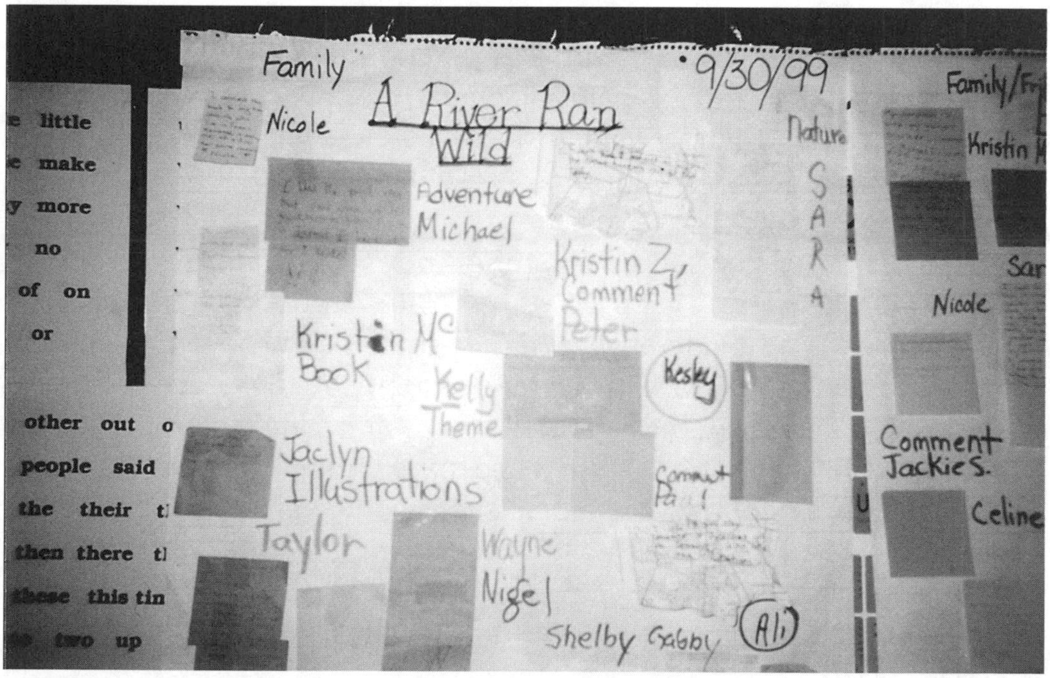

Step 8 Have students take notes while others are sharing their connections.

Have you ever observed your students' brains leaking? I'm sure you've witnessed it dozens of times when your students are staring at you with a distant gaze, their heads are perched on their hands mounted on bent elbows, and their brains are serving as a sieve rather than a focused thinking organ. Well, if you struggle with this problem like I have, this note-taking assignment will plug a few of those cerebral leaks (Power, 1998).

The note-taking process is easy and manageable. It is a tool that will help students train themselves to be attentive and focused. First, have students write the title of the book read aloud and the date as it appears on the chart in their writer's notebook (or the notebook designated to store notes). I would not isolate these notes in a separate notebook because students will soon be taking notes across the curriculum. Then have students record the category of each connection and the student's name. This will help engage them in the process while laying the groundwork for note taking. Students can refer to their notes to locate or validate information. Later "note making" will develop as students are able to organize their thoughts in their notebooks in a more personal creative way (Buzan, 1996).

Although this is an assignment for every student, I realize that at the beginning of the school year (in grades as early as third and fourth) some students may have difficulty with this part of the Connections process. For many students writing is painstaking and adding this assignment will only make matters worse. I suggest that you use your best judgment. (Also see Chapter 8, which addresses student diversity.)

The first day of school as early as third grade is the time to begin to strengthen note-taking skills by holding students responsible whenever possible to take notes. This process motivates students to be accountable for all learning and to engage in more note taking once they discover its value and manageability. To help students recognize the value of note taking, I also take notes in other related areas and share them with the students to let them know that I use this technique as well. The foundation for future note taking is laid, so support and encourage children to record the categories and students' names during the sharing part of the Connections process.

The next step is reflective in nature and will take Writing and Sharing Connections to a deeper level.

Step 9 Three times each year, graph connections and have the students write a metacognitive piece.

This is the review and assessment element of the Connections process—the point at which students look back and think about their thinking. It is during this process that students begin to take ownership of their learning. They actually begin to teach themselves, their classmates, and the teacher how and why they learn. Because this last step of Writing and Sharing Connections involves more time and effort, I will explain in detail how to graph connections and how students can write a reflective observation about the work shown on the graph (Galda, Cullinan, & Strickland, 1997; Iversen, 1996) in the next chapter.

Then, in Chapter 3, I will take you to the first Connections session of a new school year. I will show you a sampling of the connections my students wrote in a first session and how we categorized each connection and built a chart tablet page. In the remainder of the chapter, I will explain how Writing and Sharing Connections fits into our overall school year.

Supporting Learning With Connections

Writing and Sharing Connections supports learning in such a way that students operate inside the two borders of their *Zone of Proximal Development* or ZPD (Vygotsky, 1978) (see the following diagram). This is important because the best learning is done inside students' ZPD (Johnston, 1997). The learning exercises linked together during the Connections process offer students many opportunities to keep them growing from

Vygotsky's Zone of Proximal Development

potential development
ZPD (Zone of Proximal Development)
actual development

Zone of Proximal Development is the distance between the *actual developmental level* as determined by independent problem solving and the level of *potential development* as determined through problem solving under adult guidance or in collaboration with more capable peers (Vygotsky, 1978).

their actual level of development (where they are now) toward their potential level of development (independent).

Writing and Sharing Connections encourages thinking about text so that each child is able to focus on and then write what comes to mind. Theoretically, the comment on the sticky note documents a student's transaction with text (Rosenblatt, 1938/1976; 1978). I believe the Connections process embodies Rosenblatt's following statement explaining the role of "selective attention" during the act of reading:

> "Selective attention" brings some elements into the center of attention and pushes others into the background or ignores them. "Selective attention" was very important in explaining my transactional view of reading as a dynamic, fluid process in time. It helped to show that reading is a selecting, organizing, synthesizing activity. It helped to explain the back-and-forth spiraling influence of the reader and the text on the emerging meaning: the creation of tentative meanings, their influence on the possibilities to be considered for the following signs, the modification as new signs enter the focus of attention. Sometimes, as signs emerge that can't be fitted into what we have constructed, we have to look back and revise. (Karolides, 1999, p. 164)

Further, when students capture language on a sticky note in the form of a response to a content-related book, it serves as a "scaffolding" device because a relationship with a subject area is kindled through this type of free expressive writing (Vacca & Linek, 1992). *Scaffolding* is a term for cognitive assistance that supportively advances students from their actual development level to their potential development. Another scaffolding feature embedded in Writing and Sharing Connections activates when students serve as teachers: when they are engaged in discussions and in sharing connections with their classmates. Another form of scaffolding is when students are confronted with a small sticky note rather than of a blank piece of white, full-sized paper.

Chapter 2

Graphing Connections and Writing Metacognitive Pieces

When I think about how much I've learned, or how much my learning has evolved and inspired me to do more, I say to myself... What causes this? What inspires me to keep trying and to go to new levels? For me, it is my goal to succeed. I know that the power of accomplishments will be waiting for me, if I don't give up.

Where do ideas come from? Ideas develop within many minds and imaginations. My learning is like a rope with many stands [sic]. My thoughts are one stand and my classmates are the other stands. When I hear the ideas of others, I gather my own thoughts. In a way, all the strings tie together and become a rope that helps everyone climb to new levels.

Kerry

As discussed in the previous chapter, the last step in the Writing and Sharing Connections process is more involved than the others. This step—graphing connections and writing a metacognitive piece—occurs three times during the school year, which I have divided into three segments (see also Chapter 3 for more details about how Connections fits in the school year). In this chapter I outline the graphing process and explain with examples how students write a metacognitive piece.

Graphing Connections

There are several steps in the graphing process:

1. Prepare the graph for your students to plot. Review the Connections chart tablet page to the first Connections session since the last time you made graphs. If this is the first graphing of the year, go back to day one. Make a list of all book titles read aloud and the respective dates they were read. Also compile a list of all categories.

2. On graph paper, list books and their dates on the horizontal axis, and the categories on the vertical axis. Figure 5 is a sample graph form for graphing connections. Feel free to photocopy it, enlarge it, and use it with your students.

3. Make a photocopy of the graph page for each child.

4. Have students go to the chart and graph the category of their own connections for each book read. They also may refer to their notebooks for their recorded category, which is especially helpful in case a connection falls off the chart tablet. If a student was absent on a certain day, he or she may read the book read aloud that day, write a connection, and then post it on the chart.

5. Have the students review each connection they wrote.

Creating the graph is an excellent mathematics exercise for students. The graph provides a full listing of all books read, and it shows some valuable trends and tendencies for each student, such as the following:

■ In how many different categories has each student made connections? I want students to explore, take risks, and connect inside of as many different categories as possible. Remember, each category represents a mental file folder containing knowledge. It is important to open as many folders as possible and help foster growth of the knowledge inside. Connections to other pieces of literature are especially prized. When students connect one book to another through character, plot, theme, or setting, I call it an *intertextual connection*. This shows higher level thinking.

■ Which categories has each student connected with most? This can give you an indication of what each student is really interested in—one or two of those "hot buttons."

■ Which categories has each student avoided? Early in the year, I expect to see many connections in television, movies, and other nonacademic categories. As the year progresses, I hope to see a significant increase in categories that cross curriculum boundaries: literature, history, science, and so forth. When students connect the books read aloud to other literature, history studies, science, and other disciplines, some of the most powerful learning takes place.

Figure 5 Sample Form for Graphing Connections

	Categorizing My Connections								
Categories Generated Name _____									
Literature Read and Dates									

As an example, let's graph the connections written during the first part of the school year by of one of the students I track later in the book: Chelsea. Here is a list of all the categories generated from the first six Writing and Sharing Connections sessions of the school year, the book titles, and the categories that the students selected for Chelsea's connections:

All Categories

self	literature	media
family	character	place
trouble	information	science
wondering	comment	history
equal rights	question	

Book Title	Chelsea's Category
The Starry Messenger	famous person
The Librarian Who Measured the Earth	self
Looking for Atlantis	self
River Ran Wild	media
Icebergs and Glaciers	media
Dragon in the Rocks	literature

Chelsea's graph looked like the one shown in Figure 6.

Chelsea now has created a handy tool. She can use the graph to answer several questions about metacognition:

- In how many different categories have you made connections?
- Which categories have your connections fallen into the most?
- Are there any categories you would like to aim to write in during the next Connections segment?

If this is the second or final metacognitive writing of the year, I add this question:

- How have your category types changed from our last graphing to this one?

24

Figure 6 Chelsea's Graph of Connections

Categorizing My Connections							
Categories Generated				Name _Chelsea_			
Self		■	■				
Family							
Famous Person	■						
Trouble							
Wondering							
Equal Rights							
Literature						■	
Character							
Information							
Comment							
Question							
Media				■	■		
Place							
Science							
History							
Literature Read	9/4 Starry Messenger	9/10 The Librarian Who Measured...	9/11 Looking for Atlantis	9/15 River Ran Wild	9/16 Icebergs and Glaciers	9/18 Dragon in the Rocks	

Writing a Metacognitive Piece

After students graph all their connections, I have them write a reflective piece about what they have observed about their learning through the Connections process. This work is usually one or two paragraphs in length—short but very important.

At first, you might feel justified in asking what the real value is in getting students to write what I call a metacognitive piece. Why go through this process at all? Research has provided much evidence that if students describe what strategies they used to learn and then apply those strategies, they are employing metacognition (Weaver, 1994). The goal of the reflective piece is for students to gather their thoughts about the Connections process, look at where their thinking has taken them so far, and think about the directions they should consider taking as we move forward.

Pausing several times during the year for metacognition is, in one respect, a bit like completing a chapter or two in a science textbook and then pausing for a review. But there is one large difference: When students write their metacognitive pieces, I am interested in what each student comprehended from all the literature that was read aloud. They articulate their connections through this type of a reflective process so that we all gain a better understanding of new information gleaned from a variety of sources (Britton, Burgess, Martin, McLeod, & Rosen, 1975; Bruner, 1966). I am even more interested in becoming aware of how my students' thought processes are expanding, and how they are looking in more varied directions in their minds to find stored knowledge to connect to our literature. In other words, I want children to think about their thinking—a simple definition of metacognition.

I begin by having students review their graphs and all the connections they have written since the beginning of the year or since the last graphing exercise. Some of the points I ask them to consider are as follows:

- What do you think about the Connections process?
- What do you like most/least about making and sharing connections?
- As you read the connections you have written since the last graphing, how do you think you have progressed?
- How does the Connections process help you understand the book read aloud? Why?
- How might the Connections process help you understand other subjects?
- Could we set a goal or two for the next series of Connections sessions? (Here I specifically want to see students select one or two important connections categories that they have not exercised and work toward connecting to them.)

This is a challenging assignment for elementary students. The first metacognitive piece of the year is especially the most difficult one to write. Don't be surprised if your students manage to generate only a few simplistic lines. The real growth in development happens when they write the second and final pieces. As students review their connections and category graphs from the beginning of the year, you will begin to hear comments such as, "I can't believe I used to have a hard time filling up one sticky note page," and "I used to just write single-category connections, but now I write more multilevel connections." To help them begin writing the first metacognitive piece, I read aloud several benchmark pieces written by past students: one written after our first graphing session, followed by one written after our second graphing session. Presenting the first piece gives students a starting point. Showing them the second work gives children an indication of what to work toward—a sense of goal and direction.

This is the first metacognitive writing by Erin that I might read aloud:

> I like making connections because it helps me remember things I've done in the past. I also like to make connections because I get to stand up in front of my classmates and speak. I like to do that because I've got a very big mouth. One of my goals in making connections is to make more literature and experience connections.

The simple nature of Erin's first piece assures the students that this is not an impossible assignment. I would point out to my class that Erin expressed her thoughts about the Connections process after referring to her graph and set goals. I might suggest that they could include an experience that they had during Writing and Sharing Connections. I might add that it would be helpful if we knew *why* Erin wanted to make more literature and experience connections. Then I would answer any questions and facilitate a discussion about Erin's piece and how to write the first reflective piece in general.

After the discussion, I would add a challenging sense of direction to the assignment by reading Erin's second metacognitive piece:

> I like to write connections because it is a lot of fun and it helps us look at things in a whole new way. For example, in Herman Melville's Catskill Eagle [Catskill Eagle is from Chapter 96 of *Moby Dick*], we realize that if we have a "Catskill Eagle" in our souls "swooping in the deepest gorges and flying out of them again and becoming invisible in the sunny spaces" that someone's low point could be someone else's high point. I think Herman Melville in a way was trying to say that we should make

the best of our low times. In *Moby Dick*, a man got his leg bitten off by a giant whale and thus wanted revenge. I believe that Herman Melville was saying that he should look at the bright side of things and he should be saying that since he was alive and well that was all that mattered.

There is much to discuss about this second metacognitive piece Erin wrote. One of the most important facts I would point out to students is that Erin obviously did accomplish her initial goal of making literature connections in this piece connecting *Moby Dick* and Catskill Eagle. Erin has modified, expanded, and explained her ideas using specific details (Hennings, 1992). Most of my students would not be ready to produce work this insightful in our first reflective writing session. But I have found that showing them the best work of previous classes encourages their creativity.

Following this discussion students start brainstorming and collecting information for their metacognitive piece. Drawing, chatting, exploring, conferencing, and writing activities fill the room. They glean ideas from their graphs and prior connections. I encourage students to chat with one another and review the connection chart, books, and any other resources that they feel will help them.

Remember that one of the main purposes of Writing and Sharing Connections is to place students in a comfortable, nonthreatening environment and encourage them to reach deeper inside and write creatively with the knowledge they already have and the new knowledge they are grasping. In other words...to think.

After the students have had sufficient time to think and to conference with their classmates and me, the writing begins. Students share early drafts with one another and engage in peer editing before conferencing with me. Although I never require students to rewrite connections and correct grammar, spelling, or other mechanics (except in special circumstances much later in the school year), I treat their metacognitive pieces somewhat differently. I use a combination of my own coaching and peer editing to help them produce a better finished product (Calkins, 1994; Graves, 1983). (See the sidebar about peer- and self-editing.) We write during writer's workshop, and it usually takes 1 to 2 weeks to complete the metacognitive piece.

Helpful Hint

I provide the following handouts to help guide students during peer- and self-editing sessions:

- peer-editing conferring guideline
- peer-editing checklist
- self-editing checklist

An excellent source containing helpful checklists, charts, and guidelines for writing is *The Whole Language Catalog: Forms for Authentic Assessment* (Bird & Goodman, 1994).

Figure 7 Liza's Metacognitive Writing and Category Chart

Liza Schreiner

<u>How Writing and Sharing</u>
<u>Connections helps me Strenghted</u>
<u>my Learning.</u>

   Writing and sharing connections helps
me learn new words because I listen to
my classmates' connections and categories.
I also learn about my classmates and
their faimlies. I also feel good with
Dr. Wootens hand on my shoulder
because I know that noone will
laugh at me.

(continued)

Figure 7 Liza's Metacognitive Writing and Category Chart
(continued)

Categorizing My Connections

Categories Generated   Name _Liza Schreiner_

Categories Generated	9/4 Starry Messenger	9/10 The Librarian Who Measured...	9/11 Looking for Atlantis	9/15 River Ran Wild	9/16 Icebergs and Glaciers	9/18 Dragon in the Rocks	
Self							
Family				■			
Famous Person	■						
Trouble							
Wondering							
Equal Rights							
Literature		■	■		■		
Character							
Information							
Comment							
Question							
Media							
Place							
Science							
History					■		
Literature Read	9/4 Starry Messenger	9/10 The Librarian Who Measured...	9/11 Looking for Atlantis	9/15 River Ran Wild	9/16 Icebergs and Glaciers	9/18 Dragon in the Rocks	

Celebrating Our Writing

At my school, each teacher is given the job of decorating the hallway immediately outside his or her classroom. At the end of each Connections segment, my area of the hallway is decorated with our graphs and metacognitive writing. I do this as a celebration for hard work and jobs well done (Fox, 1997). On brightly colored 12" × 16" construction paper I mount a student's graph, his or her metacognitive writing, and a photo of the student. I usually have someone take a photo of each student sharing a connection in front of the class with me standing near. These compilations are displayed proudly in the hallway for all to see (see Figure 7 on pages 29–30 for an example).

Chapter 3

Connections in Progress

Writing and sharing connections helps me to learn more about the books we read aloud. I can also create mental pictures from other classmates' ideas. Also it is interesting to find out other people's points of view because each personality has a unique thought. After all of these different thoughts are put together, the story becomes more complete for me. Writing and sharing connections to books that are about history class help me to remember history facts. It offers a pocket file folder that organizes all of the information. I also think that writing and sharing connections is fun!!

Robert

Year after year I see children who have invisible battle wounds and scars from classroom and outside the classroom experiences. Some students are more crafty at masking their weaknesses, hurts, fears, and disabilities than others. Some students are not reading or writing close to grade level, while others stare at the floor with serious conflicts they brought from home or previous grades and try to suppress or act out their frustrations. I find that it is my job as a teacher-researcher to serve as a literacy learning advocate for my students (Taylor, Coughlin, & Marasco, 1997). Opening children's minds so they want to learn without fear of appearing less than perfect is dependent on their trusting me along with their classmates with their thoughts. I want children's writing to reflect what they feel in their hearts (Calkins, 1994). The first Writing and Sharing Connections session of the year begins to lay the groundwork for trust and allows me a first glimpse into my students' young minds.

Introducing Writing and Sharing Connections to the Class

The steps for conducting a Connections session were covered in Chapter 1. But because this is the first session, I will explain everything as I lead students to the carpeted area in my classroom to begin reading aloud. The book I have chosen is *Starry Messenger* by Peter Sis. I write the book title and date at the top of a fresh chart tablet page.

Starry Messenger is about Galileo's life as a celebrated inventor. His inventions and discoveries caused much excitement until the church found fault with him and sentenced him to life in solitary confinement where he became blind. Each page of the book has a time line that relates historical events to the life of Galileo. This picture book will inform social studies and science.

After reading the book aloud, I explain the concept of writing a connection to the book. I ask the students, "When you heard the story *Starry Messenger*, what did it remind you of? What did you think about?"

I read aloud several connections—both simple and more advanced—from previous years to the class. Then I have the students return to their desks, and I hand out several sticky notes. Before students begin writing, I encourage them to conference among themselves and share ideas. I want to challenge them to feel comfortable enough to fill the classroom with a literacy "sea of talk" (Britton, 1970).

After students write their connections but before they start reading them aloud, it's time to talk about our community atmosphere. I ask everyone if they have ever been laughed at. Some say yes. I ask them how it felt. We agree that it is not fun to be laughed at when you are trying your best, and we come to a class agreement: We will not make fun of one another for any reason when we are sharing our connections (Galda & West, 1995).

As a model I have written a connection to *Starry Messenger*, and I share it first. Then, the students each take that frightening first step of joining me in front of the class to read their thoughts about the book.

Here are some of the first-session connections to *Starry Messenger* from my class and the categories the class chose for them. The connections are presented as written and are not corrected:

Liza: I fell happy for Galalow because he still told people his idous when he we blind. He reminds me of Harreot tubman. (She included a drawing of Galileo looking through a telescope). (Category: famous person)

Andrew: I think that galalao was smart and he was correct. And I wonder how he became blind. I think it is fasanating that Shakespear and and galalao were born in the same year. I'm glad that galalao is right that the earth orbits the sun. (Category: wondering)

Taylor: Galieo reminds me of Erik Johnson because they both study math and phisics. (Category: famous person)

Caitlin: The Stary Mesenger Remimdd me of Marten luther King Because they were both killed for their thoughts. (Category: famous person)

Scott: The way Galilao was imprisind is like the soitery confinemet at Sing Sing. (Category: prison)

Chandni: Reminds me about when I use to look from my dad's telescope. (Category: family)

Joey: This book reminds me about my brother Alex because Galileo has stars in his eyes and my brother loves stars. (Category: family)

David M.: This book reminds me about the tme I looked through a telescope and saw Venus. (Category: self)

David R.: It reminds me the time could not sleep and I keped telling my mom I can't sleep. and she got very mad and put me in my room like I was jaile. (Category: prison)

Sara: This book reminds me of the time when I was 5 & I tried to make a teloscope to discover a new planet. (Sara drew stars around her sticky note and included a planet.) (Category: self)

Nicole: This book makes me think about when I get in trouble for not doing what my mom tells me to sometimes I get in big trouble. (Category: getting into trouble)

Kelly: Starry Messenger reminds me of Mr. Lesh because he likes stars too. (Category: famous person)

Michael: Galileo reminds me of me when I got my first telescope. Some times when I looked through I some times I saw Venus. (Category: self)

*Chelsea: this book remis me about Mr Lush how he loves to look in his teliscoup. (Category: famous person)

*Brian: This book reminds me about my nabor who is blind and he likes to read about stars and planets. (Category: famous person)

*Dawn: This story makes me think Mr. Lech is like the person in this book because he loves space, stars and planets. (Category: famous person)

(Note: Mr. Lesch is a wonderful kindergarten teacher in our school who shares his love of astronomy with his students.)

Figure 8 Chelsea's First-Session Connection

this book remis me
about Mr Lush how
he loves to look in his
teliscoup.

Chelsea

The original connections written by the last three students, Chelsea, Brian, and Dawn (indicated with an asterisk), are shown in Figures 8, 9, and 10, respectively. I have chosen these students to track later in this book, so you will see more of their work and how their writing developed.

I have included all the first-day connections from my students to help prepare you for the writing you might see in your students' first connections. Almost all of them are simple one-thought writings. However, you will be quite surprised at the increasing complexity of students' responses during the Connections process.

Using Connections Throughout the School Year

As with any methodology based on theory, there are various ways to use it in the classroom during the school year. In my classroom, Writing and Sharing Connections works in tandem with my language arts program. I implement a Book Club approach with my students similar to the literature-based curriculum set forth by Raphael et al. (1997). I

Figure 9 Brian's First-Session Connection

This book reminds me
about my nabor who is
blind and he likes to
read about stars and
Planets.

Brian

Figure 10 Dawn's First-Session Connection

This story makes me
think Mr. Lech is like
the person in this book
because he loves space,
stars and planets.

Dawn

find that the picture books and other pieces of literature that I select to read aloud during the Writing and Sharing Connections sessions strengthen not only my language arts program but also subject areas and community. This approach gives an instructional framework to read alouds in the upper grades.

I have divided the school year into three segments of Writing and Sharing Connections sessions. As mentioned in the previous chapter, I have students graph their connections and write reflective pieces after each segment. The segments are as follows:

Segment 1—the first 2 weeks of school

Segment 2—the next 3 months of school, through December 2

Segment 3—from December 3 through the end of the school year

Depending on the length of your school year, when vacations take place, and other considerations, you may decide to divide the year differently. Some teachers want students to write four metacognitive pieces, so they divide the year into four segments of Connections sessions.

I conduct two or three Writing and Sharing Connections sessions per week during the first 2 weeks of school, and then I have at least one session weekly. Sometimes I read a book and have the students write their connection during the morning. Then in the afternoon I have them share their connection, depending on the day's schedule. There are days when we have to share our connections the following day during the morning or afternoon because of assembly programs, trips, or other special events that occur during school.

The Connections sessions conducted during the first 2 weeks of school are done primarily for the following reasons:

- to introduce students to the mechanics of the process;
- to acquaint them with the idea that they are free to write and discuss whatever they think and feel about a book without fear of being laughed at or receiving a bad grade; and
- to create early samples of students' writing so that later in the year they can assess their writing development.

During the first 2 weeks of school, we usually have six Connections sessions before graphing the categories and writing our first metacognitive pieces. Because writing a metacognitive piece and categorizing connections brings about a sense of closure and understanding early in the year, students will begin to view learning reflectively and become active participants rather than passive recipients in their learning.

Students' connections during the first 2 weeks are low to midlevel in terms of mechanics such as spelling, grammar, and sentence structure. The more at-risk students are struggling a bit, and the more gifted children are beginning to realize the freedom they have to be creative in their connections. However, I am reminded regularly that once the Connections process is established, a surprisingly creative, informative, and curriculum-bridging connection can and will come from any student on any day.

At this point the confusion about literacy learning through Writing and Sharing Connections diminishes. I begin to teach more explicitly (Hancock, 1999) because every time I probe a student's connection I gain more insight into his or her learning process, which informs my teaching practices. One way it does this is by encouraging students to reach deeper and deeper into their stored knowledge and write about it on a nonthreatening sticky note. You will find that they will write about background knowledge that no test could ever uncover. And while students are writing about their stored knowledge, new knowledge will be added, or connected, to their mental filing cabinet from all the knowledge sources available in the classroom and from their own curiosity.

For now, the job of the teacher is to look for a continuous supply of literature that is enticing and content related and that makes the students *want* to read.

Our next metacognitive piece will be written in 10 weeks after the second segment and will include 9 Writing and Sharing Connections sessions. After this second segment, I observe that it is

> metacognitive ability that allows learners to transfer known information and strategies to new situations, to plan and operate strategically when they are confronted by new learning contexts, and to monitor and evaluate their attempts and adjust behavior when they are less successful than they would wish. (Wilkinson, 1999, p. 7)

During the last part of the school year, or third segment, students gain more confidence and take risks in their writing. They continue to write responses that reveal higher level thinking. We usually have 11 Connections sessions and finish the year with a final graphing and metacognitive writing exercise in the third segment.

Throughout the year, although students' connections are not graded, it is important to assess their writing development and ensure they are reaching specific learning goals. The next chapter deals with learning goals and assessment.

Following Students' Progress

As mentioned earlier, in Chapters 5, 6, and 7 we will follow the work of three students, Chelsea, Brian, and Dawn, in the Connections process as the school year progresses. These students were fourth graders who came to my class in the fall slated as low average, average, and high average students. In Chapter 8 I will highlight special education, bilingual, and gifted students who need additional guidance and challenges.

Although these students have a variety of ability levels, you will see how they develop over the school year into students who apply high-level thinking skills to respond to literature. I also believe that as their learning story unfolds through the year, you will find their progress helpful and encouraging as you work with your students.

Chapter 4

The Role of Rubrics and Learning Goals in Writing and Sharing Connections

Writing and Sharing Connections helps me really think about the books that I read. Before this year I read books quickly but when I was finished, I had no idea what I just read, but with writing connections I have to know what I read or else I won't have anything to write.

While writing connections, I have the chance to reach deep into my memory and remember my saddest and happiest moments in my life. I sometimes compare things that are totally different. Such as, once I connected the Legend of El Dorado *to the first class passengers on the Titanic because the explorers that searched for* El Dorado *were rich because they had to be in order to afford the supplies. The passengers in first class on the Titanic were also rich.*

I have the freedom of what to write and not just a specific subject. I can think outside the boundaries and write creatively. Sharing connections has also helped me a great deal. I used to be afraid of speaking in front of my class, but now I have no fears when it is my turn to share my connection.

Thomas

Students' connections are never letter graded and never fully corrected, as I mentioned earlier. My important role is to discover, appreciate, and analyze the message within the connection. This is the student's chance to share his or her voice about the text, and my job is to find value in it. To focus on correcting mechanics in this stage of the process may inflict feelings of lack of accomplishment and even failure on students who are just beginning to open up and think. However, I still analyze each connection made by a student and monitor all students' progress by using a rubric and a set of learning goals, which are both described in this chapter.

Connections Rubric

The first few Connections sessions serve as a comfortable immersion into the process that prepares students to use the connections rubric for instructive and assessment purposes. Activating the rubric lifts the Connections process to a higher level because the rubric helps clarify, define, refine, and widen each student's thinking about Writing and Sharing Connections. Students receive a copy of the Connections rubric and I invite their input throughout the school year. I make a point not to become too attached to any rubric because its purpose is to be used as an instructional tool that supports student learning and the development of higher level thinking skills and therefore is open for revision (Andrade, 2000).

The following rubric is divided into four sections. A student can earn a "3" in any or all levels. For example, a student who struggles with writing could create a design that is clever enough to earn a 3. Sometimes a connection could earn a 3 in content but not earn any points in the other categories. I never set out to score students' connections openly because the rubric and nature of the Connections process give students informative feedback about their learning. They gain an understanding about their learning process so that they can teach themselves to navigate to higher levels when they are ready developmentally.

Instructional Rubric for Writing and Sharing Connections

3

Content (Writing)

My connection is supported with the "why" and "whys."
My connection has two or more of the following techniques: intertextual links (this includes a wide range of literature such as informational books and poetry), comedy, questions (open ended), comments, opinions (personal response), skit, interview, reference to our time line, connection to history or any other subject area.

Writing Style/Organization

My connection is clearly written and well organized.

Aesthetics

My connection is pleasing to the eye and connects to the book using two or more of the following: color, originality, shape, dimension, other (such as an "explorer" connection written on sails of a ship made from sticky notes).

Mechanics
I used correct punctuation, spelling, and grammar.

2
Content
My connection is supported with the "why."
My connection has at least one of the following techniques: intertextual links (this includes a wide range of literature such as informational books and poetry), comedy, questions (open ended), comments, opinions (personal response), skit, interview, reference to our time line, connection to history or any other subject area.

Writing Style/Organization
My connection is understandable and organized.

Aesthetics
Visually, my connection is neat and reflects the book, or my connection to the book uses one or more of the following: color, originality, shape, dimension, other (such as an "explorer" connection written on sails of a ship made from sticky notes).

Mechanics
I used correct punctuation, spelling, and grammar.

1
Content
My connection does not explain "why" I made the connection.
My connection does not have any of the following techniques: intertextual links (this includes a wide range of literature such as informational books and poetry), comedy, questions (open ended), comments, opinions (personal response), skit, interview, reference to our time line, or connection to history or any other subject area.

Writing Style/Organization
My connection is not understandable and/or organized.

Aesthetics
Visually, my connection is not neat and is not visually appealing.

Mechanics
I did not use correct punctuation, spelling, and grammar.

Learning Goals

In evaluating students' connections and charting progress through the year, it is important for teachers to refer continually to a list of goals for the Connections process. The language arts learning goals I use in my classroom are gleaned from years of experience, observations, professional reading, discussions with colleagues, student input, and personal research. I consulted local, state, and U.S. national standards and learning outcomes for the social studies and science lists of learning goals (*Content Knowledge: A Compendium of Standards and Benchmarks for K–12 Education*, Kendall & Marzano, 1997). The math goals are derived from the National Council of Teachers of Mathematics (NCTM) *Curriculum and Evaluation Standards for School Mathematics* (1992). Following is a list of the language arts goals and content-specific goals I use when evaluating students' connections:

Language Arts

1. Comprehends some portion of text.
2. Fuses new knowledge with background knowledge.
   Method:
   a. Uses intertextual links.
   b. Connects subject areas together.
   c. Applies the class time line (explained later in this book).
   d. Relates experiences.
   e. Bridges media and other areas.
3. Supports the connection with an answer to the question "why?"
4. Takes notes during Writing and Sharing Connections.
5. Writes reflectively about himself or herself as a learner (metacognition).
6. Compares and contrasts.
7. Takes and defends a position.
8. Uses divergent thinking.
9. Asks and answers questions.
10. Draws conclusions.
11. Distinguishes fact from opinion.
12. Recalls content.

13. Writes the connection in the form of a letter, poem, etc.

14. Observes and relates learning to a classmate (in a positive way).

15. Regards human conditions from various perspectives.

Content-Specific Learning Goals

16. Addresses state and grade-level mandated social studies concepts under these areas:
    a. Historical
    b. Geographic
    c. Economic
    d. Civics

17. Addresses math standards:
    a. Problem solving (Standard 1 in the NCTM standards)
    b. Communication (Standard 2)
    c. Reasoning (Standard 3)
    d. Mathematical connections (Standard 4)
    e. Estimation (Standard 5)
    f. Number sense (Standard 6)
    g. Whole number operation (Standard 7)
    h. Whole number computation (Standard 8)
    i. Geometry and spatial sense (Standard 9)
    j. Measurement (Standard 10)
    k. Statistics and probability (Standard 11)
    l. Fractions and decimals (Standard 12)
    m. Patterns and relationships (Standard 13)

18. Addresses science skills, concepts, and/or issues:
    a. Makes observations.
    b. Classifies.
    c. Shows understanding of physical science.
    d. Shows understanding of earth science.
    e. Shows understanding of life science.

In Chapters 5, 6, and 7, which feature specific students and their writing development throughout the year, I list by number the goals achieved in each student connection following the analysis of each connection. Please refer back to the previous list of learning goals when reading these chapters.

Learning Goals and Standards Graphs

To better visualize the learning goals each student has achieved through writing connections, I have developed a graph to chart the goals and standards. The *learning graph* identifies the skills and/or standards a student demonstrates in each of his or her connections. It quantifies the Writing and Sharing Connections process and makes developmental evaluation visually easier. Most important, the graph provides an overview of a student's learning that informs instruction.

The graph contains a list of learning goals and standards on the vertical axis and a list of books that the students wrote connections to on the horizontal axis. Figure 11 on pages 46–47 contains a sample learning graph for graphing goals achieved by students; feel free to photocopy it and use it with your class. When a student achieves a learning goal or standard with his or her connection, it is indicated on the graph.

In Appendixes A, B, and C, graphs of the learning goals for each featured student are provided. I find that analyzing students' connections alongside these learning goals helps me assess the kind of learning that is occurring in my classroom. As teacher-researchers who do not have much time, it is important to ensure that each learning experience addresses as many subject areas as possible.

Student Self-Evaluations

As discussed in Chapter 2, I treat students' metacognitive writing differently than their connections. I have students peer- and self-edit and I hold conferences with each of them until a reflective piece is revised and edited. In addition, students read metacognitive pieces written in past years and use a rubric for self-evaluating their metacognitive pieces.

I have included the following metacognitive rubric that I developed with my students. The main advantage of having a rubric is that the expectations for writing the metacognitive piece become clearer and consequently students write a piece that has depth and is supported with details that reflect their best thinking.

Outstanding (3)—The metacognitive piece is complete.

It indicates that I have "lifted my thinking up and taken a look at how I think about my literacy experiences."

It is clearly written and mechanically correct.

Figure 11   Sample Learning Graph Form

Learning Goals/Language Arts											
1. Comprehends some text.											
2. Fuses new with background knowledge:											
a. Uses intertextual links.											
b. Connects subject areas.											
c. Applies the time line.											
d. Relates experience.											
e. Bridges media.											
3. Supports connection with "why."											
4. Takes notes.											
5. Writes reflectively.											
6. Compares and contrasts.											
7. Takes and defends a position.											
8. Uses divergent thinking.											
9. Asks and answers questions.											
10. Draws conclusions.											
11. Distinguishes fact from opinion.											
12. Recalls content.											
13. Writes connection in form of a letter, etc.											
14. Relates learning to classmate.											
15. Regards human conditions from various perspectives.											
Learning Goals/Content Specific											
16. Addresses social studies concepts:											
a. Historical											
b. Geographical											
c. Economic											
d. Civics											
Literature Read and Dates											

(continued)

Figure 11 Sample Learning Graph Form (continued)

Learning Goals/Content Specific										
17. Addresses math standards:										
a. Problem solving (S/1)										
b. Communication (S/2)										
c. Reasoning (S/3)										
d. Mathematical connections (S/4)										
e. Estimation (S/5)										
f. Number sense (S/6)										
g. Whole number operation (S/7)										
h. Whole number computation (S/8)										
i. Geometry and spatial sense (S/9)										
j. Measurement (S/10)										
k. Statistics and probability (S/11)										
l. Fractions and decimals (S/12)										
m. Patterns and relationships (S/13)										
18. Addresses science concepts:										
a. Makes observations.										
b. Classifies.										
c. Shows understanding of science.										
d. Shows understanding of earth science.										
e. Shows understanding of life science.										
Literature Read and Dates										

47

It contains supporting details that are specific.

It is descriptively written and appeals to more than one sense.

It evokes emotions.

It contains examples of my learning that let my audience know that I have learned something interesting.

I have used my imagination.

I have used descriptive language to explain my ideas.

Proficient (2)—The metacognitive piece is complete.

It indicates that I have in some way "lifted my thinking up and taken a look at how I think about my literacy experiences."

It contains a few mechanical errors.

It contains some supporting details that are specific.

It is somewhat descriptively written and appeals somewhat to more than one sense.

It somewhat evokes emotions.

It contains a few examples of my learning that let my audience know that I have learned something interesting.

I have had to use my imagination somewhat.

I have in some ways used descriptive language to explain my ideas.

Apprentice (1)–The metacognitive piece is complete.

It vaguely indicates that I have "lifted my thinking up and taken a look at how I think about my literacy experiences."

The message in the metacognitive piece is vaguely written.

It has mechanical errors but the message of the metacognitive piece is comprehendible.

It contains some supporting details that are slightly specific.

It is not as descriptively written as it needs to be and appeals to only one sense.

It does not elicit emotions.

It contains few examples of my learning that let my audience know that I have learned something interesting.

I did not use my imagination.

I have not used descriptive language to explain my ideas.

Novice (0)—The metacognitive piece is not complete or is not comprehendible.

It does not in any way reveal that I have "lifted my thinking up and taken a look at how I think about my literacy experiences."

It is not clearly written and has mechanical errors that interfere with the message of the metacognitive piece.

It contains no supporting details.

It is not descriptively written and does not appeal to any of the senses.

It does not evoke any emotions.

I did not use my imagination.

I have not used descriptive language to explain my ideas.

Meeting Curriculum Demands

With the growing pressure to meet more and more curriculum demands, I find it critical to discover ways to ensure that an integrated interdisciplinary approach is implemented. When students begin to connect subject areas under one type of lesson such as Writing and Sharing Connections, it makes the job of teaching more manageable, fun, and stimulating. And, when using the Connections process along with a system of charting students' progress with learning goals, both the increasing pressures of curriculum and assessment demands are met.

Chapter 5

Chelsea: Developing Self-Confidence in One's Voice

Chelsea is a shy, hardworking student who lacks self-confidence. Several times during the first 2 weeks of school I noticed her avoiding eye contact with me and glancing at the floor. She told me during an interview that she did not enjoy reading, and she struggled to find interesting books to read. Her third-grade year-end standardized reading test score fell slightly below grade level, which indicated she was at risk for reading failure. This was confirmed when I tested her at the beginning of fourth grade. She would have to continue to receive extra support from the reading center that operated in our school as a traditional pull-out reading intervention program. However, Chelsea and her mother met with me during the first week of school and requested that she not participate in the reading pull-out program. Chelsea said that she was embarrassed when she was called out of the room for reading and that when she returned she always felt like she had missed something important. I agreed with them, and Chelsea's mother and I spoke with the reading teacher and gained approval to release Chelsea from the reading program.

In this chapter, I have selected samples of Chelsea's writing that demonstrate her development throughout the year during the Connections program. As you will see, she gained self-confidence as a writer and in her ability to express herself and her ideas.

Following are a few of Chelsea's connections from the beginning of the school year. I briefly describe the book I read aloud in the Connections session, show Chelsea's written connection, provide an analysis of the connection along with key goals for Chelsea's continued writing development, and list by number the learning goals achieved (which are discussed and listed in Chapter 4).

The Librarian Who Measured the Earth by Kathryn Lasky

This book presents Eratosthenes, a Greek geographer, mathematician, librarian, and astronomer who measured the circumference of the Earth more than 2,000 years ago. (He was accurate to within 200 miles.) This book fuses ancient Greek history, geography, geology, and geometry with the power of story. Because Eratosthenes lived in the 3rd century B.C., questions arise during the read-aloud about the meaning of A.D. and B.C. or B.C.E., which we address when we place him on our student-driven time line. (The student-driven time line is an important Connections reference in my classroom and is discussed in the teaching idea on the next page.)

Connection: This remines me of Robert how he ask all those quashtins. It also reminds me of my sister Taylor. This a conaction to me becuase I always whont to know how big is the eath is and all those quashons (Category: self)

Analysis: Robert is our classmate who asks many questions. Chelsea is observing, connecting to, and valuing a classmate. She has observed Robert's inquisitive nature and is comparing him to a positive characteristic found in Eratosthenes. Robert was flattered that Chelsea connected to him. Chelsea has generated more than double the amount of text she wrote in Session 1 (see the first-day connections in Chapter 3) and is revealing that she listens to and comprehends text. Spelling will be addressed through personal and class word banks and spelling minilessons. Frequently used words are posted and copies are made and laminated for each child according to their needs. Students are encouraged to use environmental print and to try to spell especially the easier words correctly. I notice that Chelsea spells *reminds* correctly the second time and that she capitalizes the first word of the sentence. This is an improvement in terms of mechanics.

Key goals:

■ Continue to find ways to strengthen Chelsea's self-esteem. Give her verbal and written positive notes when the situation merits.

■ Demonstrate that what one learns in language arts can be connected to content-related areas along with her prior knowledge.

Learning goals achieved: 1, 2d/e, 3, 4, 5, 6, 14

Icebergs and Glaciers by Seymour Simon

This expository book is filled with facts that support our geography, geology, and geometry unit of study. It is important that I read and expose students to a variety of genres including informational text. I remind students that the text we are reading is similar to what they will encounter on reading tests.

Connection: This remines me of the move Titanic because of the iceberg in hit When my teacher read this book I learned that a snowflak had 6 sides (Category: media)

Teaching Idea: Connecting to a Student-Driven Time Line

One spring day one of my students said, "Did you know that Thomas Edison's light bulb was *finally* invented the same year Albert Einstein was born?" The class novel we were completing was *The Story of Thomas Alva Edison*, by Margaret Cousins (1981), and the students had recorded 1879 on our time line as the year Thomas Edison invented the light bulb. As our World War II studies began to unfold, the class decided that Albert Einstein needed to be a part of our time line because of his contributions, so his birth date of 1879 was included also, which allowed my student to make an interesting connection. The learning links that students create as a result of the time line are remarkable. Students begin to punctuate time with a wide range of events, inventions, people, and so forth. Students begin to formulate an understanding of how events shape our current society as they construct history through a student-driven time line.

Depending on the grade level, a linear time line should be made so that when an event occurs that is meaningful to students, it can be added by the students. The time line should be an actual line strung across the room. I fold an 8½" × 11" piece of construction paper in half and on one side write the year or years and then have a student volunteer to write the person's name or the event on the other side and decorate it according to its content. Because the construction paper is already folded, it is easy for the student to hang the addition on the time line like a saddle on a horse. *(continued)*

Analysis: Chelsea has related the ocean setting from the book with the movie *Titanic*. This was a popular response made by several of her classmates. Chelsea has recalled a fact that will be helpful during science and math class later. Her connection is an example of her silent language recorded on a sticky note; this type of writing is the beginning of "expressive" (Britton et al., 1975) content-related writing that is closely related to talk. During science class Chelsea shared with me that the connection she wrote helped her remember the number of sides of a snowflake. She is discovering a relationship with the topics we are studying during math and science (Medway, 1976).

Key goals:

■ Encourage Chelsea to view this book during Sustained Silent Reading and perhaps make other notes.

■ Make sure that she has time for discussions about literature with her classmates.

Learning goals achieved: 1, 2b/e, 3, 4, 6, 12

Dragon in the Rocks: A Story Based on the Childhood of the Early Paleontologist Mary Anning by Marie Day

This is the story of a young girl, Mary Anning (1799–1847), who discovers and then digs up a dinosaur. This book allows a female to be spotlighted in our history so that our time line is not totally male dominated.

Connection: This remines me of when I was going to New Jersy we say 2 gyes that were wilking around in the street and selling prophns [telephones] but they were broken phons. This remins me of when we read the story about galileo and when we read *The Libarian who Measured The earth* because they both ask a lot of austan [questions]. (Category: experience)

Analysis: Chelsea's connection that links *The Librarian Who Measured the Earth* and Galileo to Mary Anning illustrates that she is capable of thinking beyond the comprehension level. She links together literature creatively through common threads she finds on her own. In terms of spelling, my class reminded me that in the past they have memorized spelling words (or other information) for a test and then quickly forgot them so that they could make room for the next batch of spelling words, which has happened in Chelsea's case with the word *reminds*. I try to address this issue by having students continually check their spelling.

Remember, connections are not graded. Students use the rubrics and the Connections process to instruct themselves developmentally. If I graded students' connections, I feel that I would be stunting their growth as writers. Moreover, students are able to retrieve what they have learned during Writing and Sharing Connections even though I do not test them often. Not testing motivates students to value and enjoy the Connections process so they do not forget what they have learned. I have administered traditional quizzes on the content from the Connections sessions read-aloud books, and the students recalled facts from the texts successfully.

Learning goals achieved: 1, 2a/d, 3, 4, 6, 12, 18a/d

Teaching Idea (continued)

The bank of knowledge that the time line presents shows up constantly in students' writing. Exploring history and developing the time line visual, students begin to construct learning through the inquiry method. They begin to teach themselves. This type of child-driven learning engages students to become active participants in their learning process while they assume ownership of their learning (Langer, 1992).

Other Time Line Possibilities

Time lines can start as early as pre-Kindergarten. Students could develop a time line using the 12 months, and below the appropriate month student birthdays and holidays can be added. A linear time line used in addition to a calendar helps students understand sequencing as it relates to them.

As we study U.S. history, the names of our presidents and the years of their terms in office find a place on the time line. As we uncover events that happened during various presidential administrations, we form a "chain" of these events under the president.

Another time line idea is to add favorite authors' birthdays. If you assign an author study, the copyright dates of the books the author has published can be placed on a time line. This exercise could lead to discussions about how the author has changed over the years, what characteristics have remained the same, the author's style, or other patterns that are noticed.

The time line in my classroom is shown in the photo on page 54.

Chapter 4 details my system for charting students' learning goals after each of the three Connections segments during the year. In Appendix A is Chelsea's learning goals graph for the beginning of the year. Most of the goals she achieved are basic, as can be expected for many students when they first begin writing connections.

As discussed in Chapters 1 and 2, students write metacognitive pieces three times a year that reflect their thoughts on their connections. Here is Chelsea's first metacognitive piece, based on the connections she wrote at the beginning of the school year (see also Figure 12 showing Chelsea's connections category chart and her original writing):

Writing and sharing connections makes me understand the book better because the teacher reads it and we write a short response about how it connects to us or our families. I understand the story better because I write about the story and then I share it. It makes me smarter. It also helps me face my fears of standing up in front of people.

Figure 12 Chelsea's First Metacognitive Writing and Category Chart

Chelsea Spallon-e

Writing and sharing Connections makes me understand the book better because the teacher reads it and we write a short response about how it connects to us or our families. I understand the story better because I write about the story and then I share it. It makes me smarter. It also helps me face my fears of standing up in front of people.

Categorizing My Connections

Categories Generated   Name __Chelsea__

Categories Generated	9/4 Starry Messenger	9/10 The Librarian Who Measured...	9/11 Looking for Atlantis	9/15 River Ran Wild	9/16 Icebergs and Glaciers	9/18 Dragon in the Rocks	
Self		■	■				
Family							
Famous Person	■						
Trouble							
Wondering							
Equal Rights							
Literature						■	
Character							
Information							
Comment							
Question							
Media			■	■			
Place							
Science							
History							
Literature Read							

55

Analysis: Although Chelsea's metacognitive piece appears to be primitive, it addresses three important features of Writing and Sharing Connections: reading aloud books, writing expressively, and providing a secure environment for learning. Chelsea opened her metacognitive piece stating that reading aloud helps her understand the story. I am depending on reading aloud to strengthen Chelsea's comprehension skills (Bruce, 1983; McCormick, 1977; Michener, 1988; Wells, 1986) so that she can begin to experience success as a reader and as a test taker in reading. I hope other skills will improve during read-aloud sessions such as familiarity with story components that include character and theme (Feitelson, 1988; Morrow, 1988). In this piece, Chelsea also is endorsing the value of expressive writing (Britton et al., 1975).

So far Chelsea has let me know through her metacognitive piece and connections that she lacks self-confidence. This is important for me to learn so that I can continue to focus my instruction on helping her realize her potential.

Chelsea's following connections were written during the middle of the school year in response to the books *Polar the Titanic Bear*, *Encounter*, *The Sign of the Beaver*, and *Sir Cumference and the First Round Table*.

Polar the Titanic Bear by Daisy Corning Stone Spedden

This book is about a young boy named Douglas living during the Edwardian Era. It is based on a true story and told through the eyes of Douglas's toy bear. The story culminates with their tragic voyage on the ship Titanic. Although this book is not directly related to the content we are studying, I read it aloud because the students have requested it. This book includes primary sources such as family photographs and a photo of an actual ticket stub from Titanic.

Connection: This remines me of the time I had mizal [measles] and I whent to the shool and every body there had the mizals and it was so weird because everbody had dots on them. I also remember when it winter and I was playing in the snow with titanic and she said that she remembers it. My sister when she was little and she was fluffy and small that she felt like a teddy Bear. This also reminds me of the book called Icebergs and glachers. It also reminds me of my great grandma because when she was about one or two years old she could goen on the Titanic. (Category: literature and self)

Analysis: Chelsea is opening up. Chelsea wrote about the measles because the character in the story also had the measles. She describes them as dots, and the book describes them as spots. Chelsea compares her winter experience with

56

titanic (her toy) and her sister to the hostile freezing water where the Titanic sank. Her intertextual link to *Icebergs and Glaciers* was remotely anticipated because she connected that book to the Titanic a few weeks ago. She reaches a little deeper in her knowledge base and mentions that her grandmother is old enough to have traveled on Titanic. I asked Chelsea how she arrived at this comment, and she said that she subtracted her grandmother's age from our current year. Then she compared that number to the year the Titanic sank (1912). By doing this, Chelsea met several math standards (16b, 17a/b/h, 18a). Chelsea is constructing a time line that is real to her because she connected her grandmother mathematically to the Titanic and consequently to the book that was read aloud. Also note that Chelsea wanted to place her connection into more than one category.

Learning goals achieved: 1, 2a/b/c/d/e, 3, 4, 6, 10, 12, 16a/b, 17a/b/h, 18a

Encounter by Jane Yolen

The story in this picture book is of a native boy who dreams that strange and frightening people will come to his island. He tries to warn everyone about these strangers but no one will listen. When Columbus and his men arrive, they give the natives trinkets in exchange for gold and other valuables. And when Columbus departs, he takes the native boy. The boy escapes and dives into the ocean to swim to freedom.

Connection: **This book remines me of when I had a wied dream about everything up side down and I was walking upside down, I also like this book because I like how he makes me realy go in the dream with him. I also like the drawings because he makes you really see what the people looked like and also made me see what the sharp pole looked like. I thought it was wrong when they took the people to their country. I also connect this book to my story because how I tell about everything and how I feel. (Category: comment)**

Analysis: Chelsea is relating her dream to the dream of the young native boy. Chelsea lets us know that she transacted with the text when she says that "he makes me go in the dream with him." She states her opinion about the treatment of the natives at the hands of the explorers. During writer's workshop Chelsea had just written a story that has a dreamy setting and has connected it to this book. The story she wrote was so moving that another student was inspired to write a poem that he dedicated to her.

Learning goals achieved: 1, 2a/d, 3, 4, 6, 7, 10, 12, 16d, 15

The Sign of the Beaver by Elizabeth George Speare

We used this historical fiction novel as a class novel. This trade book describes the northeast during the 1700s through the eyes of Matt, a 12-year-old who must survive in the wilderness without his family.

Connection: This reminds me of when my sister and her fiends made a big mess in my room and did not clean it up and I had to clean it up and also when I split a jar of milk and I was on the table and I was pouring it in my cereal and the milk dropped. Also when I lost my favorite best friend's necklace. (Category: self)

Analysis: Chelsea shows good comprehension by responding to two episodes in the book. The first one is when a bear went into Matt's cabin and trashed it, and the other one is when someone stole a gun from Matt. One goal for Chelsea is to clarify her connections with a little more information from the book to support her response.

Learning goals achieved: 1, 2d, 4, 6

Sir Cumference and the First Round Table: A Math Adventure
by Cindy Neuschwander

Geo of Metry, a carpenter, was appointed to build a table for King Arthur of Camelot and his knights to sit around at meetings. He tried various shapes for his table and, of course, settled on a round table. His son, Radius, helped with some of the mathematics.

This picture book is worth reading to your students even if it does not fit into your history unit of study because it contextualizes math geometrical terminology in a fun, inquisitive adventure during the Middle Ages. A continuation of this mathematical saga can be found in *Sir Cumference and the Dragon of Pi: A Math Adventure* by the same author.

Connection: This reminds me of the vikings because they had all weird names like Snorrie and all those names. This also reminds me of Gutinbirg because he had to work hard just like the carpinter. But Gutinburg worked harder. But Go [Geo] was told to do work that wasent used. (Category: book)

Analysis: The connection to the Vikings (which we read about in our social studies book) is clear in Chelsea's response. The rest of her response deals with the level of effort used in order to complete a task. Her spelling is improving but still contains many inconsistencies such as in the words *reminds* and *weird*.

Learning goals achieved: 1, 2b, 3, 4, 6

At this point in the school year—after the second set of Connections sessions—I chart students' learning goals again. Chelsea's second learning graph (found in Appendix A) shows that she is achieving a few more difficult language arts goals and some content-specific goals. Students also write another metacognitive piece at this time. Here are Chelsea's reflections about her writing development in the middle of the year:

Writing and sharing connections has helped me face my fear of speaking in front of people. It also helped me to write more and it helped me to not be as nervous when I share my ideas about something in front of my classmates. In the past when I got a writing assignment I would get scared when I saw that big sheet of blank paper facing me. Now I look forward to writing because the post-its made it fun and easy. Now I can't wait for writing time so that I can fill up blank sheets of paper and then share my pieces with my classmates. I hope I get my piece published soon!

Analysis: Every year I feel as though there are some students who suffer from lack of confidence. Chelsea is one of these students. Again, boosting her self-confidence is a priority. The good news is that writer's workshop is one of her favorite times of the day. Her latest story inspired another student to write a piece of poetry that he dedicated to her. This event boosted her self-confidence in an authentic way—from her peers. Chelsea is gaining more confidence as a writer because she has almost filled her writer's notebook with stories, content-related notes, poems, and other entries. She is writing to learn and therefore learning to write. It is clear that her connections and other writing pieces are improving in terms of content and mechanics. (See Figure 13 for Chelsea's second category chart and metacognitive piece.)

During the last part of the school year, I hold nine Connections sessions. Following are two of Chelsea's writing samples and her final metacognitive piece.

Figure 13 Chelsea's Second Metacognitive Writing and Category Chart

Writing and Sharing Connections

Writing and sharing connections has helped me face my fear of speaking in front of people. It has also encourged me to write more and helped me to not be as nervous when I hare my ideas about something in front of my classmates In the past when I got a writing assignment, I would get scared when I saw   that big blank sheet of paper facing me. Now I look forward to writing because the post- its make it fun and easy. I can't wait for writing time so that I can fill up blank sheets of paper and then share my pieces with my classmates. I hope I get my piece published soon!

Chelsea Spallone

Categorizing My Connections

Categories Generated   Name _Chelsea Spallone_

Categories Generated	9/21 Polar the Titanic Bear	10/6 Follow the Dream	10/10 Encounter	10/14 Sign of the Beaver	10/28 Gutenberg	11/12 Sir Cumference...	11/16 Erasmus	11/24 Eating Plates	12/2 Rough-Face Girl
Self	■			■					
Family									
Tragedy									
Learning									
Discovery									
Observation									
Literature	■			■	■			■	■
Character									
Example						■			
Comment		■		■			■		
Question									
Media									
Point of View									
Experience									
History									
Country		■							
Literature Read									

The King's Day: Louis XIV of France by Aliki and *"The Eclipse,"* a poem by Jaques Prevert, translated by Lawrence Ferlinghetti

This book and poem are about King Louis XIV (the Sun King) who ruled France for 72 years (1643–1715). Every event of this monarch was celebrated, from his *Lever* (his morning ritual) to his *Coucher* (his going-to-bed ceremony). The book and poem look at the king's eccentricities in riveting detail.

Connection: In the poem The Eclipse I compare Louis XIV to the sun because both are big and Powerful. I also compare that one dark night when Louis the Sun King disappeared to an eclipse when the sun also disappears. (Category: comparison)

Analysis: Chelsea's comparison of Louis XIV to the sun indicates that she comprehended the text. Chelsea took a risk when she wrote the Roman numeral for 14, and I complimented her for including this mathematical detail correctly in her connection. Chelsea's second sentence shows a higher level of understanding because she had to apply her understanding of a solar eclipse to King Louis XIV's disappearance. She has bridged social studies, math, and science: Touching the history standard is obvious because of the book's content and Chelsea's connection about the King; the inclusion of the Roman numeral covers a math standard; and the science Earth-related standard is achieved when Chelsea mentions the eclipse.

This connection was a breakthrough for Chelsea in terms of mechanics. Her spelling and sentence structure also were much improved.

Learning goals achieved: 1, 3, 4, 6, 8, 10, 12, 16a, 17f, 18a/d

The Princess and the Peacock Or, the Story of the Room by Linda Merrill and Sarah Ridley

Based on a true story, this book is about the famous artist James McNeill Whistler who was commissioned to paint a great design on the walls of a room in the home of Frederick Leyland. However, Leyland was unsatisfied with Whistler's masterpiece. The "Peacock" room that Whistler painted for Leyland was dismantled and reconstructed in the Freer Gallery of Art at the Smithsonian Institution. I want students to know that rejection is sometimes a part of pursuing your dreams, a theme that is found in many books.

Connection: I connect to myself because when I think something will be perfect it usually is the opposite. I connect it to <u>the Painter and the Wild Swans</u> because they both enjoyed painting birds.

I connect this book to myself because whenever I think something I did is great someone else always has something to say about it and it makes me feel like what I did was not good enough for that person. I also connect this book to tj because he also painted birds. (Category: famous people)

Teaching Idea: Creating a Content-Related Poetry Anthology

I have students purchase a three-ringed binder and then decorate the cover and write in bold letters "Poetry Anthology" along with their names. I punch holes in the photocopied poems I have selected for the students to include their anthologies. When I hand out a poem to students, we read the poem and engage in a discussion. Sometimes I include photocopied pages about the history of the author. We also perform the poem in a multitude of ways, including doing choral readings, acting out the poem, and doing "snapshots" (sometimes called statues), in which students stand like statues illustrating a scene or feeling derived from a poem. Afterward, I assign students to write a response on the back of the photocopied poem and on the front draw an illustration.

Writing a response to poetry is another way to elicit students' background knowledge about the poem so that they can begin to think about the poem in a deeper way. This method fosters divergent thinking and lifts thinking above comprehension by connecting something in the poem to other areas of our lives. For example, Kerry wrote this connection or response to "The Road Not Taken" by Robert Frost: "This poem reminded me of my trip to Florida because my family was driving and we made one wrong turn and we were driving the wrong way for an hour." *(continued)*

Analysis: Chelsea, along with most of her classmates, made the connection between Whistler and Teiji (tj) in *Painter and the Wild Swans* (Clement, 1993; another book I read aloud during this segment of the year). Her other connections continue to confirm her low self-confidence. But she has come very far with mechanics in this connection. Her spelling and sentence structure are much improved from the beginning of the year as well.

Learning goals achieved: 1, 2a/d/e, 3, 4, 5, 6, 7, 8, 10, 12

Here is Chelsea's end-of-the-year metacognitive writing:

Writing and Sharing Connections has strengthened my learning skills. This method has improved my spelling and other writing related mechanics along with developing my imagination. It has permitted me to feel brave and confident. When I share my creative piece in front of the class I don't feel timid inside because I have Dr. Wooten's support right beside me. Writing and sharing connections has taught me more about peers and how they think. I think of writing and sharing

connections as a demonstration of creative learning tied together in one big family. Writing and sharing connections is an organized chart filled with color and interesting shapes. I learned that writing on post-its makes it fun and easy. Now, because of writing and sharing connections, I can't wait for writing time.

(Chelsea's end-of-the-year metacognitive piece, along with her graph, is shown in Figure 14.)

Analysis: Writing and Sharing Connections has provided a way for Chelsea to process her thinking on paper. The thinking documented on sticky notes has given me a manageable means to support her learning while providing her with a challenging learning environment. During the year there were two important types of learning happening simultaneously for Chelsea: One was instruction based on her needs and the other was an opportunity for her to challenge herself creatively and know that she was a vital contributor in our learning community. When Chelsea exposed a skill that needed attention, instruction came from different sources such as my direct intervention, other classmates' ideas, and reading and listening to books (which helped me manage all the needs in the classroom). Furthermore, I know that listening to all the other students' connections that demonstrated comprehension of literature acquainted Chelsea with story grammar and other features of text. This in turn prepared her for other books that she would encounter.

All the class expected Chelsea to succeed, and more important, Chelsea expected herself to succeed. Being pulled

Teaching Idea (continued)

In another example, James was able to pull together in a sophisticated approach his knowledge of literature and history in response to a poem. We had just completed the novel *Back to the Day Lincoln Was Shot* (Gormley, 1996) along with other related literature. One of the several poems we had studied and maintained in our poetry anthologies was "O Captain! My Captain!" by Walt Whitman. I read the picture book *Polar the Titanic Bear* (Spedden, 1994) and asked students to write connections. James wrote this connection:

> This reminds me of the poem "O Captain, My Captain." Abe Lincoln is the "Captain" who survives the terrible Civil War. The line "O Captain, My Captain our fearful trip is done," means that many people have lived through the Titanic when many others have died. But "Heart! Heart! O the bleeding drops of red, Where on the deck my Captain lies fallen cold and dead." This means that the family thought that everything was all right because they survived the Titanic tragedy but then the son was killed in an auto accident. Just how Abe Lincoln thought that everything was all right but unexpectedly he was shot and killed by John Wilkes Booth.

Before we began studying King Louis XIV and the historical turmoil of his time (religious persecution that precipitated an exodus to the new world), I had students add the poem "The Eclipse" to their poetry anthologies and used it as an introduction. We were also studying Roman numerals at the time. Louis XIV gives students a practical application for knowing how to interpret Roman numerals. I also added Louis XIV to our time line (1638–1715). We revisited the poem during this unit in conjunction with the picture book about King Louis XIV for connections.

Figure 14 Chelsea's End-of-the-Year Metacognitive Writing and Category Chart

Metacognative
Piece

Writing and Sharing connections has strengthened my learning skills. This method has improved my spelling and other writing related mechanics along with developing my imagination. It has permitted me to feel brave and confident. When I share my creative piece in front of the class I don't feel timid inside because I have Dr. Wootens support right beside me. Writing and sharing connection has taught me more about peers and how they think. I think of writing and sharing connections as a demonstration of creative learning tied together in one big family. Writing and sharing connections is an organized chart filled with color and interesting shapes. I learned that writing on post-its makes it fun and easy. Now, because of writing and sharing connections, I can't wait for writing time.

BY CHELSEA SPALLONE

Categorizing My Connections

Categories Generated   Name ___Chelsea Spallone___

Categories Generated	(12/10/98) Legend of El Dorado	(1/21/99) The Kings Day	(2/4/99) Sir Francis Drake	(2/23/99) The Pirate Queen	(3/4/99) Painter & the Wild Swans	3/24/99) The Tower of London	(4/15/99) Pizarro's Death	(5/11/99) Thomas Edison	(5/19/99) Tower of London II	(6/99) Princess and the Peacocks	(6/99) Samuel's Choice	(6/99) The Hatmaker's Sign
Famous People			■	■				■				■
Intertextual Link											■	
History							■					
Media												
Subject												
Comparing		■										
Experience												
Inquisitive												
Artist												
Comment						■			■			
Self	■									■		
Literature Read												

64

out of class and taken to the reading lab several times each week in years past isolated her from the place she needed to be to feel successful. I have to give credit were it is due: Chelsea deserves the applause. All she needed was the right support and learning environment. She worked hard. She wrote to learn and learned to write (Martin, 1987; Mayher, Lester, & Pradl, 1983). Her writing during writer's workshop had voice, imagination, emotion, and self-confidence. She read to learn and therefore improved as a reader. And now Chelsea is no longer labeled as an at-risk student because she scored in the 96th percentile on the end-of-the-year standard reading test. She also achieved many higher level language arts learning goals and some content-specific standards during the third segment of Connections (see Appendix A). Chelsea did it.

Chapter 6

Brian: Gaining Motivation to Read Through Writing

Brian is regarded as a leader among many of his peers, and he participates in discussions. He also scores well on tests. At the beginning of the year, Brian's lack of interest in reading took several weeks to uncover. He was reluctant to discuss this with me. He did admit that he liked series books such as the Boxcar Children and did not like the class novel we were reading. Brian also told me that our school library and my classroom did not have any books that he would like.

Following I have selected three connections Brian wrote at the beginning of the year before attempting his first metacognitive piece.

***The Librarian Who Measured the Earth* by Kathryn Lasky**
As summarized in the previous chapter, this book presents Eratosthenes, a Greek geographer, mathematician, librarian, and astronomer who measured the circumference of the earth more than 2,000 years ago.

Connection: This book reminds me of my mom because she loves all kinds of math and geography. She likes to read and I learn more and more to me. She is just like Erathosthenes. (Category: famous person)

Analysis: Comparing Brian's first connection (in Chapter 3) to this one indicates that he is comprehending text but has not used higher level thinking skills when writing his connection. I predict that once he observes higher level thinking skills modeled for him by his classmates (as they share their connections) he will begin to write with more depth.

Key goal:

■ Model a connection for Brian that exhibits higher level thinking skills.

Learning goals achieved: 1, 2d, 3, 4, 6

Looking for Atlantis **by Colin Thompson**

This is one of the most imaginative books recently published. Its open-ended story plot is about a young boy's journey in search of Atlantis. The detailed art work has readers searching for clues that might help the boy find his destiny. My students postulate that this author purposely adds details in his artwork that remind us of artists such as Escher, Graham Base, and others. The illustrations and story strengthen our explorers unit of study because we vicariously endure hardships, adventure, disillusionment, and discovery.

Connection: This book reminds me of the books *I Spy* because in *Looking for Atlants* you have to look for things and in *I Spy* you have to look for things these two books are very alike. (Category: intertextual link)

Analysis: The intertextural links are just starting to appear in Brian's connections. This type of connection is unlocking Brain's potential for writing a response with depth.

Key goals:

■ Strengthen Brian's sense of community.
■ Encourage him to enjoy reading and writing.

Learning goals achieved: 1, 2a, 3, 4, 6

River Ran Wild: An Environmental History **by Lynne Cherry**

This is the true story of the Nashua River's history. Following the arrival of European settlers in the 1600s, who treated the river differently from the Native Americans who inhabited the area first, the river became so polluted that it began to die. Fortunately a series of recent events has restored and cleaned the river so that it flows with life again. The river's history is conveniently told in the form of a time line on the book's endpapers. Each page of the story has a different border that strengthens the time period being depicted.

Connection: This reminds me of my camping trip because the beach was puluted then two days later it was clean and clear and there was no garbage I thought the rangers picked all the up. (Category: self)

Analysis: Brian wanted his connection to be categorized as "self" rather than "experience" or "trip." When he refers to "*my* camping trip" he visits the book through his eyes or self. Although my first reaction was to encourage him to change his category, I wanted to allow him to visit this book through his "self." His connection reveals that he has comprehended the story. The class also has gotten to know Brian a little better because of his camping story.

Learning goals achieved: 1, 2d, 3, 4, 6

Here is Brian's first metacognitive piece (see also Figure 15):

Writing and sharing connections helps me to understand my classmates and it also helps me to understand what the author of the book is trying to say about his or her book. I learn about history because we read about Galileo and Eratosthenes. Before writing and sharing connections I didn't even now they existed.

Analysis: Brain's metacognitive piece demonstrates the effectiveness of students as teachers. He has brought to my attention indirectly that he prefers auditory learning. This is not uncommon except Brian is excellent at it. He mentions in his metacognitive piece that he gains information about books from students' responses to books and from books read aloud. Unfortunately, I have uncovered Brian's closely guarded secret: He does not enjoy reading and skillfully avoids reading whenever possible. His metacognitive piece points out that his main reason for reading is to find out what the author wants him to know. I hope that in a nurturing way I can tell Brian that one of my primary goals is to help him find literature he will enjoy. He should not be ashamed of his lack of enthusiasm for reading. The time to lead this bright young man to some books that will lure him to read is now.

In Appendix B are Brian's three learning graphs from the year. The graph from the first segment of connections shows that he is achieving basic language arts learning goals at this time.

I have selected the following three connections Brian wrote during the middle of the year to demonstrate his further writing development. The books he responded to include *Follow That Dream*, *Gutenberg*, and *Eating the Plates* before writing his second metacognitive piece.

Follow the Dream: The Story of Christopher Columbus by Peter Sis

This book is about the life of Christopher Columbus. It tells of his dreams as a young boy and how he attained his dreams during life. The book includes a replication of a map from 1492 with a time line of Columbus's voyages.

Figure 15 Brian's First Metacognitive Writing and Category Chart

Brian Stern

<u>Writing and Sharing Connections</u>

   Writing and sharing connections helps me to understand my classmates and it also helps me to understand what the author of the book is trying to say about his or her book. I learn about history because we read about Galileo and Eratosthenes. Before writing and sharing connections I didn't even know they existed.

Categorizing My Connections

Name _Brian Stern_

Categories Generated	9/4 Starry Messenger	9/10 The Librarian Who Measured	9/11 Looking for Atlantis	9/15 River Ran Wild	9/16 Icebergs and Glaciers	9/18 Dragon in the Rocks	
Self				■			
Family		■					
Famous Person	■						
Trouble							
Wondering							
Equal Rights							
Literature			■		■	■	
Character							
Information							
Comment							
Question							
Media							
Place							
Science							
History							
Literature Read	9/4 Starry Messenger	9/10 The Librarian Who Measured	9/11 Looking for Atlantis	9/15 River Ran Wild	9/16 Icebergs and Glaciers	9/18 Dragon in the Rocks	

Connection: This book reminds me of a book called *The Great Christopher Clumbus* because they are both about him. This book also reminded me of the time I got my first telescope. This book also reminded me of the time I saw a picture of the tall ships that were coming into glencove. This book also reminded me of the time I got a ship that I made In a bottle nobody thought I could do it but I did. This book also reminded me of the time I whent to the beach and I saw a lot of boats. It also reminded me of the time I went to a pool party and there was a remote controled boat. (Category: book)

Analysis: Brian's intertextual link to an informational book about Columbus included the reason why he linked them together. One goal for him was to write a more specific reason for linking two books together. Because "teaching is a guided tour around demonstrations" (Fox, 1997), I will continue to model and point out examples of connections that will help Brian add depth to his writing.

Several students including Brian discovered that Columbus did not use the telescope because it had not yet been invented. Students made this discovery because we were reading about Columbus and Galileo and studying about them in social studies. The students elected to add both men to our student-driven time line (which is explained in the teaching idea in Chapter 5). Brian remembers class discussions that we had during our first few days of school.

Learning goals achieved: 1, 2a/d, 3, 4, 6

Gutenberg by Everette Fisher

While telling the story of Gutenberg getting his printing press operating and patented, this book also addresses his personal life and the struggles and hardships he endured.

Connection: When the printing press was made Galileo wouldn't have been born for 110 years. When John Gutenburg died Galileo was 4 years old. In my mind history is a chain one loop connect to the next also in Colonial Williamsburg we went to the printing shop and they showed us how the printed a long time ago. (Category: famous person)

Analysis: Brian used the time line and math calculations to connect Galileo to Gutenberg. He has met history and math standards, and he has gained a clearer understanding of history. Brian's definition of history is imaginative. He provided me with a lens into his thinking and I am impressed. In time, Brian's writing mechanics will improve.

Learning goals achieved: 1, 2b/c/d, 4, 5, 6, 8, 10, 16a, 17a/b/d/h, 18a

Eating the Plates: A Pilgrim Book of Food and Manners **by Lucille Recht Penner ("Bugs for Dinner," Chapter 1)**

This informational book is about how and why the Pilgrims ate what they ate. It is full of trivia that makes everyone wince and want more. For example, while the Pilgrims were travelling across the ocean aboard their ships, some preferred to eat after dark so they couldn't see the bugs crawling over their food. This is a great book to read around Thanksgiving.

Connection: This book reminds me of a report I did about the Mayflower. The book was called "If You Sailed On the Mayflower" This book also reminds me of the time I went to the Liberty Science Museum and on the top floor there was a plan for the May flower and they let us make boats in a bottle. (Category: book)

Teaching Idea: Creating an "Explorers" Unit of Study
Using Poetry as an Introduction

Along with the book *Follow the Dream* (Sis, 1991), I include a poem titled "The Things That Haven't Been Done Before" by Edgar Guest in our explorers unit of study. Students place this poem in their poetry anthologies (see the teaching idea in the previous chapter about creating a poetry anthology). Following the introduction, reading, and discussion of this poem, we discuss future challenges and then substitute some of our challenges with the ones in the poem.

We focus on the question, How are Columbus's challenges different from the ones we have today? To spark our discussion, I add the following quote from Frances Hodgson Burnett, author of *The Secret Garden*, who overcame obstacles of poverty, writing for publication, the death of her son, and more. I also point out that she lived about 400 years after Columbus.

> At first people refuse to believe that a strange new thing can be done, then they begin to hope it can be done and all the world wonders why it was not done centuries ago.

Using the Time Line in Social Studies

Columbus (1451–1506) is added to our time line during our explorers unit (see the teaching idea about the time line in Chapter 5). We study Columbus's fourth trip to the New World; an excellent resource is the textbook *First Americans* by Joy Hakim.

The fact that European explorers were willing to kill for the gold and other riches from the New World is a conceptual umbrella that covers social studies concepts such as economy (scarcity, money, and values), history (time), geography (location), and civics.

(continued)

Teaching Idea (continued)

Tying in Science to the Explorers Unit

Exploring aspects of the metal gold is one way to bridge subject areas in a study of Columbus. I have students acquaint themselves with the periodic table by subtracting the atomic weight of silver (107.868) from gold (196.967). Other related questions include the following:

Which element is heavier?

Which one has the largest atomic number?

What determines the value of elements such as gold (Au) and silver (Ag)?

The atomic number of Silver (Ag) is 47 and gold (Au) is 79. Are the atomic numbers odd or even? Are the atomic weights odd or even?

Are these numbers prime and/or composite? Why?

Examining spices is another way of connecting subjects. I place several different spices in test tubes. For example, you can use cinnamon, nutmeg, pepper, curry, dill, parsley, or mint. Studying properties of these spices, such as smell, color, shape, and taste to detect their identities will support science standards. Comparing salt and sugar is a lesson that also will bridge science and social studies.

It is fun to allow students to use one sense at a time. Blindfold students and have them put their hand into a container with various spices for them to identify. They may use any sense except sight.

Related questions to ask include the following:

Why did the Europeans want spices so badly?

What were their uses?   *(continued)*

Analysis: Brian's book and trip experience is reflective of what I read aloud, but he needs to explain his linking method more clearly. I encouraged him to do so. He relates science and history together, which sparks an interest to start a boat-making project to enhance our Thanksgiving holiday celebration. I'm also beginning to detect an improvement in Brian's writing mechanics.

Learning goals achieved: 1, 2a/d, 3, 4, 6

Here are Brian's second metacognitive piece and my analysis of his writing development after the first two thirds of the school year:

Writing and sharing connections has helped me dig deeper into my thoughts and share my best thinking about a book. I know that no one will laugh because Dr. Wooten is by my side. It helps me to respond to a book in a smart way and in a way that my classmates understand. This has changed my learning by teaching me to put a big idea on a little post-it. It might not be a lot of text but it is high quality work. I am interested to see what will happen or is going to happen in my classmates' lives because of writing and sharing connections.

Analysis: Brian is proud of all the books and knowledge he has collected during the past 3 months of school. He feels smart and knows he is growing. Moreover he is not afraid to take risks. How? One way is that he seized the moment and on his own wrote a skit about an explorer titled *Funny Old History*. Although most everyone would find it entertaining, our class knew all the historical facts that Brian converted into humorous pieces of the skit. When he performed it for the class, he included some of his classmates as actors and actresses. He wrote this skit during writer's workshop and at home. Brian has discovered that learning comes from private affairs such as writing a skit as well as through social interactions gained when the skit was performed. (See Brian's metacognitive piece and category chart in Figure 16 on page 74).

Teaching Idea (continued)
Tying in Math to the Explorers Unit

To connect math to our unit, I ask students to work on the following questions, based on our time line:

How long did Christopher Columbus (1451–1506) live?

Could he have used the telescope? Why or why not?

How many years ago was Columbus born?

After this second segment of connections and metacognitive writing, I graphed the learning goals that Brian achieved again (see the graph in Appendix B). He is beginning to achieve goals in all the content areas with his writing responses, and I continue to encourage him.

During the last part of the school year, Brian's writing ability developed even more. He began to demonstrate higher level thinking skills and more indepth writing, as shown in his following final connections.

The Legend of El Dorado: A Latin American Tale, written and illustrated by Beatriz Vidal and adapted by Nancy Van Laan

Versions of this South American legend have been responsible for luring generations of explorers in search of riches. *El Dorado*, which literally means *the gilded one*, is based on a story recorded by a Spanish conquistador from a Columbian Indian around 1541. The story is about a king who covered his body with gold dust and dived into Lake Guatavita where his wife and daughter disappeared into the arms of a serpent. Each year the king repeated this ceremony in hopes of being reunited with his wife and daughter. And, each year the King's people threw treasures into the lake as well. For years this ceremony at Lake Guatavita occurred until one year the king did not return from his dive. Legend concludes that he was then reunited with his wife and daughter.

Connection: *The legend of El Dorado* **reminds me of a book my sister brought me a book that was in all Spanish it was an ancient legend that had been going on in Spanish history for centuries. My sister showed me**

Figure 16 Brian's Second Metacognitive Writing and Category Chart

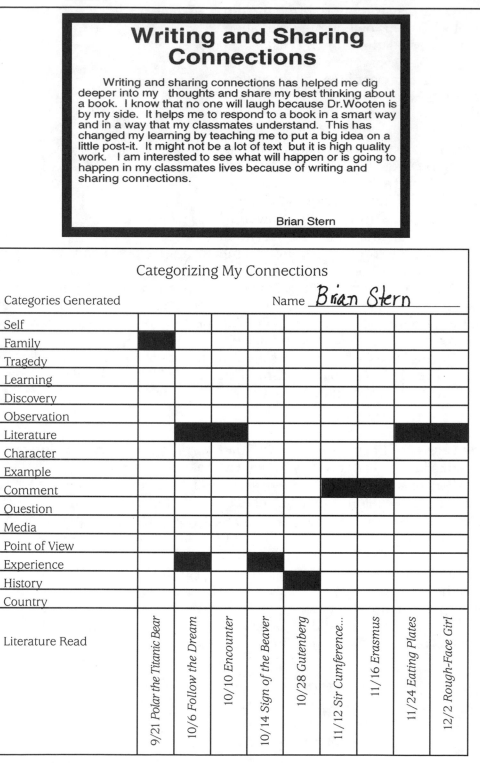

Writing and Sharing Connections

Writing and sharing connections has helped me dig deeper into my thoughts and share my best thinking about a book. I know that no one will laugh because Dr. Wooten is by my side. It helps me to respond to a book in a smart way and in a way that my classmates understand. This has changed my learning by teaching me to put a big idea on a little post-it. It might not be a lot of text but it is high quality work. I am interested to see what will happen or is going to happen in my classmates lives because of writing and sharing connections.

Brian Stern

Categorizing My Connections

Categories Generated   Name *Brian Stern*

Categories	9/21 Polar the Titanic Bear	10/6 Follow the Dream	10/10 Encounter	10/14 Sign of the Beaver	10/28 Gutenberg	11/12 Sir Cumference...	11/16 Erasmus	11/24 Eating Plates	12/2 Rough-Face Girl
Self									
Family	■								
Tragedy									
Learning									
Discovery									
Observation									
Literature		■	■		■			■	■
Character									
Example									
Comment							■	■	
Question									
Media									
Point of View									
Experience		■	■	■					
History					■				
Country									

Literature Read

74

a picture of a lake that looked like a rainbow. The lake reminded me of the lake in the book. When the book says treasure it reminds me of my second cosin because she owns a gift basket business and one of the gift basket disins is a treasure chest that has gold everything gold chocolate, gold sparkles and the gold sparkles remind me of how every year the king would put gold all over himself to remind the serpent about the kings family and my second cousin is my family. When the Queen and princess walk away to the river and then are gone that reminds me of the time I was in the 'Roosevelt field Mall with my family when I get water from the water foutin and then I turn around my family is not there then they come back and I am reunited with my family just like the King and his family. In the book when Dr. Wooten read the part in the book with the little poem it reminds me of Doug's poem that he wrote because both poems were short but they both meant a lot. When the King dives into the water, it reminds me of the time I first learned how to dive in my aunts pool. El Dorado took place in 1541 and Christopher Columbus was born in 1451 but if you turn the four and the five around in the year the place you get the year Christopher Columbus was born and visa-versa and this book reminds me of our social studies because they both say what the name Eldorado and they have the story. When the book says the serpent eyes that were made of rubies it reminds me of a ring that my sister gave me that looked like rubies. When the book says the Indians were worth the treasure it reminds me of how my mom says how nothing can by me not even 100 treasures and that makes me feel good just like how when the King got reunited with his family. I think of my other cousin because he likes to scobba dive and he might scubba dive in a lake. (Category: inquisitive)

Analysis: Brian has experienced a real breakthrough with this connection. Only 3 months of school have passed and Brian is writing a connection that lets us know that he is comprehending text, exhibiting high-level thinking skills, linking various subject areas, and achieving at least one standard under every core subject area. His connection is a valuable assessment tool that informs my instruction. Because we all listen to his connection at one time, he is modeling his writing for his classmates to learn, which makes my job easier.

Developmentally this connection is much better than his others. He used all the ways he experimented with writing connections earlier in the school year. In September Brian's connections related to people close to him with the following (refer to Brian's metacognitive chart in Figure 16):

Starry Messenger to his blind neighbor (9/4)

The Librarian Who Measured the Earth to his mother's love of learning and reading (9/10)

River Ran Wild to a camping trip with his family (9/15)

Then Brian started tying books to his connections with *Icebergs and Glaciers* (9/16) to *Snow Birds*, and *Dragon in the Rocks* (9/18) to *Under the Dirt*. Later, he connects *Encounter* with two books, and at the end of October, he creates math connections with famous people such as Galileo and Gutenberg. Then, for the next several weeks, Brian's connections alternate between family and books.

The connection to El Dorado is an example of how a story can reach a student and transact in a way that lifts the learning bar, or achievement level. Did Brian comprehend, recall details, infer, and predict? The answer is yes. He also reached a higher level of thinking when he interfaced his thoughts with the book. He, along with the other students, can recall text and let us know it while using higher level thinking skills. Reading worksheets and working in workbooks tend to take the challenge and fun of learning away from the students and the teacher. Brian used the tools he collected with Writing and Sharing Connections to transact and conceive text. It has taken 16 Connections sessions for him to show that with one connection he can achieve all the learning goals and standards listed following. He is breaking down subject barriers and making my job easier while lifting the level of expectations higher for all of us.

Teaching Idea: Using Poetry With *The Legend of El Dorado*

I use the poem entitled "El Dorado" by Edgar Allen Poe in addition to reading the picture book *The Legend of El Dorado* (Van Laan, 1991). Students place this poem in their poetry anthologies.

Adding to the Time Line

Two time line additions are made with this poem: 1541 for the legend of El Dorado, and 1809–1849 for the poet Edgar Allan Poe.

Tying in Math

There are some subtraction problem possibilities related to the timeline.

Using Science

Because gold is one of the treasures said to have been thrown into Lake Guatavita, I ask students why it is regarded as such a precious metal. This is a good research project for a student who enjoys challenges and riches. Also, students may want to find out what 14-carat gold means.

Learning goals achieved: 1, 2a/b/c/d, 3, 4, 5, 6, 8, 10, 12, 14, 15,16a/b/c/d, 17b/d/h/m, 18a

The Pirate Queen by Emily Arnold McCully

This is an informative story based on the life of the female Irish pirate Grania O'Malley who lived approximately 1530–1603. She fought through life with a sword, doing the things that pirates did. Unusual is the fact that she once met Queen Elizabeth I of England.

By this point in the school year, my students have become watchdogs for historical events that correspond to or overlap with one another in some way. After reading *The Pirate Queen*, one student checked the time line and found that both Queen Elizabeth I and Grania O'Malley died in the same year.

Another picture book you might want to make available is *The Ballad of the Pirate Queens* by Jane Yolen (illustrated by David Shannon).

Connection: Everyone thinks Queen Elizabeth is so nice but she did some really mean things.

> **Dear Elizabeth,**
> **Yo, chill out stop being jealous. You know this would not have happened if you didn't use all that lead make-up! Now he thinks that you are ugly.**
> **From your future,**
> **Brian D. Stern**
> **(Category: famous people)**

Analysis: Students are beginning to write connections in the form of letters and poems. They are experimenting with different voices and perspectives as well. I especially like the formal way in which Brian signed his name to his letter.

Brian's comments about lead make-up and the queen's looking ugly are significant coming from a boy who said he hated to read. He has been reading on his own, searching for the reason Queen Elizabeth did not marry. One theory was that she wanted to remain neutral with other world powers. But the students focus on another theory. Evidently, Queen Elizabeth had scars on her face from small pox. The fashion of the day was for ladies to smear a white, lead-based make-up on their faces. This the queen did, and she punctuated the look with little blue lines drawn in the make-up to simulate veins.

Learning goals achieved: 1, 2, 3, 4, 6, 7, 8, 11, 12, 13, 15, 16a/b/c/d, 18a/c

Samuel's Choice **by Richard Berleth**

This historical fiction text is set during the American Revolution as the Battle of Long Island rages in Brooklyn. The protagonist is a 14-year-old African American slave who makes a choice to help during the war rather than run for freedom.

Connection: I connect *Samuel's Choice* to *Katie's Trunk* because they both are about the Revolutionary War. They also about a choice to go back to the house or stay with her family. Samuel had a choice to stay and help or to leave to safety. (Category: subject)

Analysis: Brian links these two books together because they both are set during the Revolutionary War. He also sees a similarity between characters in the two books. What is not revealed in the connection is the fact that Brian read *Katie's Trunk* on his own: a good sign from a student who professed to hate to read at the beginning of the year.

Learning goals achieved: 1, 2a/d, 3, 4, 6, 9, 10, 12, 16a

Here is Brian's end-of-the-year metacognitive piece:

Writing and Sharing Connections has helped me to think brilliantly because I am listening to what my classmates have to say and think about a book. This process is fun because we transform the post-it that we write on into a different shape. Writing and Sharing Connections has become an exciting event that I look forward to. Dr. Wooten plays classical music in the background so our brain's thinking process moves faster so that we think better. I think I am smarter because I have been writing and sharing connections this year.

Writing and Sharing Connections has motivated me to write down what I think. It has motivated me to write when I am not writing and sharing connections. I used to be afraid when my teacher said "Writing Time" because I never got ideas. I looked around and everyone was writing but me. Writing and Sharing Connections has gotten me to think about a book and then it can be pictured in my mind.

(Brian's end-of-the-year metacognitive piece, along with his graph, is shown in Figure 17.)

78

Figure 17 Brian's End-of-the-Year Metacognitive Writing and Category Chart

Metacognitive Piece

Writing and Sharing Connections has helped me to think brilliantly because I am listening to what my classmates have to say and think about a book.This process is fun because we transform the post -it that we write on into a different shape. Writing and Sharing Connections has become an exiting event that I look forward to. Dr. Wooten plays classical music in the background so our brain's thinking process moves faster so that we think better. I think I am smarter because I have been writing and sharing connections this year.

Writing and Sharing Connections has motivated me to write down what I think. It has motivated me to write when I am not writing and sharing connections. I use to be afraid when my teacher said "Writing Time" I never got ideas. I looked around and everyone was writing but me. Writing and Sharing Connections has gotten me to think about a book and then it can be pictured in my mind.

Brian D.Stern

Categorizing My Connections

Categories Generated   Name _Brian Stern_

Categories Generated	(12/10/98) Legend of El Dorado	(1/21/99) The Kings Day	(2/4/99) Sir Francis Drake	(2/23/99) The Pirate Queen	(3/4/99) Painter & the Wild Swans	(3/24/99) The Tower of London	(4/15/99) Pizarro's Death	(5/11/99) Thomas Edison	(5/19/99) Tower of London II	(6/99) Princess and the Peacocks	(6/99) Samuel's Choice	(6/99) The Hatmaker's Sign
Famous People												
Intertextual Link	■				■		·			■		
History		■				■						
Media												
Subject												
Comparing												
Experience						■						
Inquisitive												
Artist												
Comment				■								■
Self	■		■					■	■			
Literature Read												

Analysis: Brian's three metacognitive pieces have mentioned the positive effects of community. He realizes and has stated metacognitively that he learns from his classmates. It was shortly after a classmate wrote a connection in the form of a poem that Brian wrote his connection in the same genre. He did the same with writing a letter as a way to respond to literature. He is observing his options and experimenting with them. His best attempt was the skit he wrote as an extension of a connection written earlier in the school year. He learned very quickly that writing requires a lot of time and hard work. He selected classmates to be actors and actresses under his leadership as the producer, and he learned that directing a play with his classmates had some difficulties as well. Some of the students who were actors and actresses were not as pliable as he had hoped, but in spite of the difficulties Brian was successful.

Brian showed me another glimpse into his potential with his connection to *The Legend of El Dorado*. Although it contained mechanical problems, it was a reflection of a whirlwind of thinking. In this piece he related to books, family, a classmate's poem, and the time line. We were able to visit Brian while discovering more about *El Dorado*. Two responses in his connection that merit mentioning are Doug's poem and the dates 1541 (El Dorado) and 1451 (Columbus's birth year) because he described their processes in his metacognitive pieces.

Brian's connection to *El Dorado* achieved social studies, math, and science standards as well as high-level reading and thinking skills. And, although he achieved more complex language arts learning goals with most of the responses he wrote during the third segment of the Connections process, he did not achieve many content area learning goals. (See Brian's learning graph in Appendix B.)

Brian somewhat avoids the actual writing and reading processes. He masks his avoidance with music and artistic shapes made from sticky notes. What does this mean? Brian is smart and has not yet let me know where he wants to go with reading and writing. I believe he is touching, but not embracing, his potential metacognitively. I believe that Brian wants to be perfect; he would do very well if he had a fill-in-the-blank approach to writing. Writing is a revealing and frightening task that has a sense of permanency because it is documented on paper. Brian and other students may wonder, What if I make a mistake? What if I can't write creatively? What if I misspell words? In spite of all the support of classmates, Brian is still concerned about revealing too much about his literature learning. Brian is a sharp thinker and wants to be successful in school. But he continues to tell me even a year after leaving my class that there are other things he would rather do than read.

Chapter 7

Dawn: Expressing One's Voice on Important Issues

Dawn is quiet and hardworking. She informed me during an interview that she enjoyed reading Beverly Cleary and Roald Dahl books. Dawn always participates during Sustained Silent Reading. When she completes an assignment early she is quick to pull out her book and read. She looks forward to our library visits so that she can check out a book.

As you will see from the following connections, Dawn used writing to voice her opinions on a variety of social and political issues. She also managed the mechanics of writing well. And, throughout the school year, her writing improved greatly.

Here are two of Dawn's connections I selected from the first part of the year. (Note: Because I selected some of the same Connections sessions to showcase in the previous chapters with Chelsea's and Brian's writing, I have not repeated the summary of the read-aloud books here.)

The Librarian Who Measured the Earth by Kathryn Lasky
This book, summarized in Chapter 5, presents Eratosthenes, a Greek geographer, mathematician, librarian, and astronomer who measured the circumference of the earth over two thousand years ago.

Connection: I do not agree with this book because I think that girls and boys should be treated equaly. I also think ths book is very interesting beacause he studied so many subjects. (Category: equal rights)

Analysis: The fact that girls were not allowed to attend school in Greece 2,000 years ago is why Dawn elected to share her position about gender equality. Dawn is allowing her imagination to unravel gender biases based on her knowledge (Johnston, 1997). Dawn is taking risks and is developing higher level thinking skills. I predict that Dawn will soon realize that our time line will be male dominated. Her strong position is a good model for her classmates to observe.

Learning goals achieved: 1, 2e, 3, 4, 6, 10, 15

Teaching Idea:
Tying in Math and Other Content Areas With *The Librarian Who Measured the Earth*

Along with the book *The Librarian Who Measured the Earth*, I read the poem "Arithmetic" by Carl Sandburg (1955) to students because it is lighthearted and relates to math and numbers in a fun, straightforward, and creative way. Students place this poem in their poetry anthologies. We also add 3rd Century B.C. to the time line and study the terms A.D. and B.C.

Using Math

Eratosthenes calculated the circumference of the earth (his calculation differs from today's accepted circumference by only 200 miles). My students and I first estimate then measure the circumference of our heads.

It is said that Eratosthenes may have used a grapefruit to work on his formula for calculating circumference. Mentioning this fact provides an opportunity for a study of Fibonacci numbers. A good source for this lesson is *Math Wizardry for Kids* (Kenda & Williams, 1995).

Using Science

Math and science have a lot in common. Herophilius (a physician mentioned in *The Librarian Who Measured the Earth*) lived during the same time period as Eratosthenes. Checking one's heart beat and pulse might be a fun exercise.

Also from this time period was Ctesobius who invented the first water-driven clock and the first keyboard musical instrument. Here are two more opportunities for lessons in sound and time.

Looking for Atlantis by Colin Thompson

Summarized in the previous chapter, this book is about a young boy's journey in search of Atlantis.

Connection: This book reminds me of the *Eye Spy* books. On every page theres something new to see. The pictures are so colorful. They just get more and more interesting. (Note: Dawn used a neon orange sticky note to emphasize the "colorful" in her connection.) (Category: intertextual link)

Analysis: Based on Dawn's and other students' writing, we are going to need to have a minilesson during writer's workshop about "breaking open words" such as interesting, good, fun, and others (see the sidebar teaching ideas on the next page). For example, if a student describes a book as interesting, I try to have him or her tell exactly what is interesting about it. One goal this year is to encourage my students to support their opinions with details while describing them with descriptive language.

Learning goals achieved: 1, 2a, 3, 4, 6

Here are Dawn's first metacognitive piece and my analysis (see also Figure 18 on page 84):

Writing and sharing connections has helped me because I am not afraid of standing in front of the class when I share my ideas. When Dr. Wooten's hand is on my shoulder I have confidence. I really like writing and sharing connections. I think it's a good way to share how you connect to the book. You don't even have to connect to the book. It can be someone or something else. I think Dr. Wooten's idea of w&s connections is a good idea.

Analysis: I believe Dawn's lack of self-confidence is not a result of poor reading scores or lack of enjoyment of reading, but because she is discovering herself as a learner through depth and diversity. Writing and Sharing Connections helps construct a strong sense of community that uncovers and celebrates diversity. Every time Dawn shares her connection, she heightened our social awareness. And, this happens with every student. Soon we discover that our diversity can bring us closer together. Dawn is a forerunner in this process. Her comments about women's rights required her to connect to a small part of the story and then take a stand about the rights of all people. Dawn's concerns about social issues will help bring about a more respectful and reflective learning atmosphere.

Dawn's learning graph from the first segment of Connections sections can be found in Appendix C. The graph shows that she is already achieving more complex language arts standards and a few science learning goals.

During the middle of the year, Dawn continued to voice her opinions in writing. The following connections I selected to include in this chapter are written in response to the books *Follow the Dream*, *From Hand to Mouth*, *Eating the Plates*, and *Rough-Face Girl*.

Teaching Idea: Breaking Open Words

I use questions such as these to teach students how to "break open words," or further explain in detail and support statements:

- What is interesting (describe)?
- Why is it interesting?
- How is it interesting?
- Where is it interesting?
- When is it interesting?
- Which senses make this (literature) interesting?

Answering one or more of these questions helps students write more descriptively without being overwhelmed.

Figure 18 Dawn's First Metacognitive Writing and Category Chart

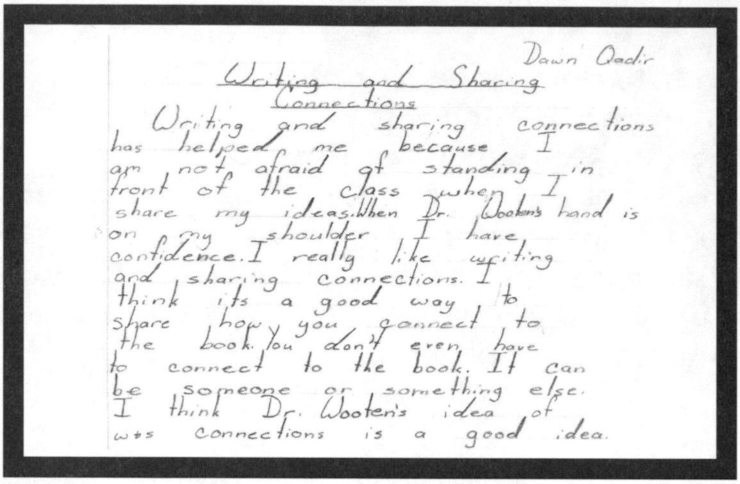

Dawn Qadir

Writing and Sharing
Connections
Writing and sharing connections has helped me because I am not afraid of standing in front of the class when I share my ideas. When Dr. Wooten's hand is on my shoulder I have confidence. I really like writing and sharing connections. I think its a good way to share how you connect to the book. You don't even have to connect to the book. It can be someone or something else. I think Dr. Wooten's idea of w+s connections is a good idea.

Categorizing My Connections

Name **Dawn Qadir**

Categories Generated	9/4 Starry Messenger	9/10 The Librarian Who Measured...	9/11 Looking for Atlantis	9/15 River Ran Wild	9/16 Icebergs and Glaciers	9/18 Dragon in the Rocks	
Self							
Family	■						
Famous Person							
Trouble							
Wondering							
Equal Rights		■					
Literature			■			■	
Character							
Information					■		
Comment							
Question				■			
Media							
Place				■			
Science							
History							
Literature Read							

Follow the Dream: The Story of Christopher Columbus by Peter Sis
This book is summarized in the previous chapter.

Connection: This book reminds me when I didn't want to go to school. Now I am greatful I go to school because I made new friends including teachers and students teachers. This book also reminds me of when I'm scared any time beacause I think Chris was scared but he was as brave. (Category: experience)

Analysis: Dawn is channeling her imagination to link personal emotional experiences to Columbus's voyage. She is pointing personal emotional pathways into history so that she can relate better to Columbus. Overcoming fear opens the door to bravery. The fact that Dawn ended her connection with the word "brave" indicates a deeper understanding of the appreciation of bravery.

From Hand to Mouth or, How We Invented Knives, Forks, Spoons, and Chopsticks and the Table Manners to Go With Them by James Cross Giblin
I share an excerpt from Chapter 3 (pages 30–32) of this book that briefly discusses Erasmus's *Civility in Children*, a book published in 1530 about table manners for a young French prince who later became King Henry II. Proper etiquette included these rules: "Don't pick your nose while eating and then reach for more food" and "Don't clean your teeth with your knife." It certainly isn't difficult to hold the interest of fourth graders with tidbits like that from the 1500s!

Connection: This book reminds me of my dad because he comes from Pakistan. In Pakistan they have all these messy foods. They have weird names too. Their foods look like different things. Even though their foods might not look scrumsous. Once you take a bite the food is good. They eat with their hands. They take this kind of bread and pick up a pece of food with it and and then they eat it. I also do this. Even if it may seem like bad table manners. Thats how they were brought up. (Category: country)

Analysis: Dawn has permitted us to have a glimpse of her family's background. I can notice improvement in her mechanics as the young writers continue to focus on content.

Learning goals achieved: 1, 2d, 3, 4, 6, 15

Eating the Plates: A Pilgrim Book of Food and Manners by Lucille Recht Penner ("Bugs for Dinner," Chapter 1)

This informational book, summarized in the previous chapter, is about how and why the Pilgrims ate what they ate.

Connection: This book reminds me of Ismile, he helps my dad work outside. The reason this book reminds me of him is because of his religion he left his home land too. Not because of his religon but because it is a better place work here in America instead of Pakistan. (Category: famous person)

Analysis: In her connection, Dawn moved past the disgust of what the Pilgrims ate when they were sailing to America, and chose to respond to why the Pilgrims left their homeland. She has the ability to look intuitively beyond what is going on to discover why it has happened.

Learning goals achieved: 1, 2d, 3, 4, 15

Rough-Face Girl by Rafe Martin

This picture book is an Algonquin Cinderella story. David Shannon captures the Native American lore in the illustrations. A question that students ask after viewing this book is, "Why are there tepees in this book when we learned that the Algonquins on Long Island lived in wigwams?" Another picture book I sometimes use in conjunction with this one is *Sootface: An Ojibwa Cinderella Story*, retold by Robert D. San Souci.

Connection: This book remindes me of my mom because she would buy gifts for my cousins when they would visit and I would feel bad if she did not buy me a gift. This connects to the step sisters and their father....because he gave them beautiful clothes so that they could meet the chief's son who was single. The Rough faced girl did not get any nice clothes from her father because he did not have any money or nice clothes left. (Note: This

connection was written on strips of sticky notes and stuck together to make a necklace similar to the beaded necklaces worn by Native Americans.)(Category: family)

Analysis: Dawn's comparison to her own feelings of being left out means she is empathizing with the rough-faced girl. Dawn continues to be drawn to the emotional element of story. Her turning the paper she wrote on into a necklace is actually another type of connection to the story. She took a chance in doing it, and I applauded her.

Learning goals achieved: 1, 2d, 3, 4, 15

Here are Dawn's second metacognitive piece and my analysis:

Writing and Sharing Connections has helped me with lots of things. Now I am not afraid to stand up in front of my classmates and read. I love it when Dr. Wooten puts her hand on my shoulder because it gives me confidence and courage. Writing and sharing connection has made me more creative because whenever someone reads me a story, usually something pops into my head that the book reminds me of. Now I get to jot it down after I hear the story. I also like Writing and Sharing connections because what we connect to also reflects to the time line. This method helps me think more creatively and now I pay more attention to books because I know that I am learning more in a fun way.

Analysis: Writing and Sharing Connections is a form of expressive writing and can yield great benefits only when it is done in a low-risk environment so that each response is valued, accepted, questioned, and explored but never criticized (Vacca & Linek, 1992). This means that my students and I must be supportive of every student. Dawn and her classmates know this and have sometimes said that they have so many connection ideas pop into their heads that they have to make decisions about which ones they should write. I call this "mental editing."

Writing and Sharing Connections holds content close to the writing process. Our class time line (described in Chapter 5), which Dawn refers to in her response, provides a tool that helps Dawn and her classmates synthesize and structure their knowledge so content area writing is not a regurgitation exercise but one that will have a creative and fun dimension. (See Figure 19 for Dawn's original metacognitive writing and category graph.)

Figure 19 Dawn's Second Metacognitive Writing and Category Chart

Dawn

     Writing and Sharing Connections has helped me with lots of things. Now I am not afraid to stand up in front of my classmates and read. I love it when Dr. Wooten puts her hand on my shoulder because it gives me confidence and courage. Writing and sharing connection has made me more creative because whenever someone reads me a story, usually something pops into my head that the book reminds me of. Now I get to jot it down after I hear the story. I also like Writing and Sharing connections because what we connect to also reflects to the time line. This method helps me think more creatively and now I pay more attention to books because I know that I am learning more in a fun way.

Categorizing My Connections

Categories Generated   Name **Dawn**

Categories Generated	9/21 Polar the Titanic Bear	10/6 Follow the Dream	10/10 Encounter	10/14 Sign of the Beaver	10/28 Gutenberg	11/12 Sir Cumference...	11/16 Erasmus	11/24 Eating Plates	12/2 Rough-Face Girl
Self				■					
Family								■	
Tragedy	■								
Learning									
Discovery									
Observation									
Literature									
Character									
Example									
Comment									
Question									
Media			■						
Point of View									
Experience		■							
History									
Country							■		

During the first two thirds of the school year, Dawn's writing ability, creativity, and higher level thinking skills have developed more based on her increasingly complex connections. She is using a variety of perspectives in her responses, and, although she is not attaining many content-specific standards, Dawn is achieving language arts learning goals (see the learning graph in Appendix C). She is able to understand and reflect about social studies concepts such as change and empathy. Dawn is an example of a student who would recall factual information in a traditionally structured test successfully.

Dawn continued to write complex responses with good mechanics in the final third segment of the year. I chose the following connections—based on the poem "Sir Francis Drake," the essay "After the Funeral," and the book *The Hatmaker's Sign*—to show Dawn's further writing development.

"Sir Francis Drake: His Daring Deeds" by Roy Gerrard

Written in the form of quatrain, this poem tells of the adventures of Sir Francis Drake, from "when he was ten and went to sea with grown up men," to when he became the daring knight who led the way for the defeat of the Spanish Armada in 1588.

Connection: I liked this book so much I decided to make up my own rhyme that relates to him.

> Sir Francis Drake, What a man,
> I do not think he had a tan.
> He made himself famous I say,
> and drove the spanish king away.
> He fancied a Queen oh so thin,
> her nic name must have been "pin".
> Aboard his ship he had a cat
> and dove into the ocean to save him
> imagine that.
> Aboard each ship there was a cat
> to eat all of the mice and rats.
> I must end this poem about this famous man
> and thank you class for listening again.
> This book was fun. It inspired me to write my
> own poem. I am glad Dr. Wooten shared this
> book with us. (Category: history)

Analysis: This is the second time Dawn has taken a chance and broken from the traditional form in writing a connection. Earlier in this third segment of Connections she responded with a connection written as a letter to King Louis

XIV. She handled both connections very well. Responding in verse happens at some point every year. When the first student writes a connection in verse, shares it aloud, and gains my generous approval, many more poems follow from other students.

Learning goals achieved: 1, 2a/d, 3, 4, 5, 6, 7, 8, 10, 12, 13, 15, 16a

"After the Funeral: Francisco Pizarro"

I read this essay (pages 101–102) from *Uncle John's Giant 10th Anniversary Bathroom Reader* (Bathroom Readers' Institute, 1997). (I shelve this book with my personal books because it is geared for an adult audience.)

Pizarro, who was responsible for bringing the potato to Europe, was stabbed to death during an argument about the Inca riches stolen in 1541. Pizarro was one of the thieves. During the following 350 years his remains were moved repeatedly for various reasons, and for a while his remains were misplaced. It took a forensic expert to conclude which remains were the real Pizarro. Finally, in 1984, 443 years after his death, he was laid to rest in a glass sarcophagus in Peru.

Connection: I can't believe that Pizarro died sort of like Magellan died because when Magellan was in the Philippines to claim land one of the Filipinos threw a spear and it hit Magellan and he was stuck in the sand. Then his crew ran off because they didn't want to die like Magellan. I also connect this book to *Walk Two Moons* because when Sal's grandma died her body was flown back to Bybanks, Kentucky. Pizarro's was flown to a museum.

Dear Mr. Pizarro,
I have noticed that you died like Magellan. You were both stabbed. I know you discovered the potato and I am proud of you for that, but I do not like your rude behavior. I am eating many potatoes in memory of you. *Sir Francis Drake was born 2 years after you died.*
From,
Dawn
(Category: letter)

Analysis: The many facts covered by Dawn in her comments and letter are far reaching. She makes an excellent connection to Magellan, remembers the significance of the potato, and mentions a thought from *Walk Two Moons*, a novel she read on her own and responded to in her response log. Dawn's mechanics are very good, even when building some complex sentences.

Learning goals achieved: 1, 2a/b/c/d/e, 3, 4, 6, 7, 8, 10, 12, 13, 15, 16a/b/c

The Hatmaker's Sign: A Story by Benjamin Franklin retold by Candace Fleming

This story is based on a true conversation between Benjamin Franklin and Thomas Jefferson. Franklin told Jefferson a story about a hatmaker who listened to suggestions about what to include on a sign for his store. If the hatmaker had heeded all the advice he was given about his sign, there would have been no sign left to display. This story was told to encourage and give wisdom to Jefferson when representatives from the 13 U.S. colonies were revising and editing The Declaration of Independence that Jefferson wrote.

Connection: I connect this book to *The Princess and the Peacock* because the man Whistler was painting for did not like his work but he stuck with his work anyway. I also connect this book to the movie *Titanic* because Rose wanted to marry Jack not the man she was engaged to and she got her way. I also connect this book to Scott because he will keep bugging Dr. Wooten until he gets what he wants. I also connect John to Rifka in *Letters from Rifka* because they will not let her out of this place in America and be with her family just because of the way she looks but she does get out. I also connect this book to women's rights because women kept on fighting and finally they got the same rights as men. I also connect this to Christopher Columbus because he wanted so much to sail to the new World and finally he got the chance too. All these people that I just menchaned all fought for what they wanted and they got their way. They fought for their opinion and I think I would too. If I were in their perdicament. What is important is they believe in their selves. (Category: famous people)

Analysis: All the rights that Dawn believes in come forth in this response. Her support of her thinking with intertextual links, a movie, a classmate experience, and a famous person all add up to being a self-actualized person, and according to Maslow and his hierarchy of needs, she is at the top.

Learning goals achieved: 1, 2a/b/c/d, 3, 4, 6, 7, 8, 10, 12, 14, 15, 16a/b/c/d

Following are Dawn's end-of-the-year metacognitive piece and my analysis:

Writing and Sharing Connections has opened my mind to things that put my thoughts to new challenges. Now I think more creatively in every subject. This method lets us have fun while we connect to our own lives, learn new things about our classmates and understand what we are reading. This method also lets people share their ideas and opinions no matter what other people think! When my peers share, I learn new things because they help me imagine things in a different way. Before Writing and Sharing Connections I was not as motivated as I am now. Writing and Sharing Connections has motivated me to put more effort into my work and many other things. Writing and Sharing Connections has given me a chance to share my thoughts with the whole class. When I share my ideas I know someone is listening to what I have to say no matter if they like it or not. I also like this method because after someone shares, you are allowed to say if you agree or disagree with the person who has shared. Connections has given me more confidence in sharing my thoughts not only with classmates, but also with other people. I think Connections has also made me a better writer because now I think I add more detail to my work. Now I believe my imagination, my creativity and my effort all have improved because of Writing and Sharing Connections!

(Dawn's end-of-the-year metacognitive piece and her category graph are shown in Figure 20.)

Analysis: Dawn discusses the positive impact and need for a strong community in all three of her metacognitive pieces. Community was the multifaceted dimensional ingredient she needed to encourage her thoughts about her learning. She has gained confidence from knowing that her work reflected her best effort and that I, along with her classmates, am cognizant of her achievements. Students observe her and follow because this shy young lady has leadership qualities. She enjoys reading and writing and it shows. She is able to use

Figure 20 Dawn's End-of-the-Year Metacognitive Writing and Category Chart

My Metecognitive Piece

Writing and Sharing Connections has opened my mind to things that put my thoughts to new challenges. Now I think more creatively in every subject. This method lets us have fun while we connect to our own lives, learn new things about our classmates and understand what we are reading. This method also lets people share their ideas and opinions no matter what other people think! When my peers share, I learn new things because they help me imagine things in a different way. Before Writing and Sharing Connections I was not as motivated as I am now. Writing and Sharing Connections has motivated me to put more effort into my work and many other things. Writing and Sharing Connections has given me a chance to share my thoughts with the whole class. When I share my ideas I know someone is listening to what I have to say no matter if they like it or not. I also like this method because after someone shares, you are allowed to say if you agree or disagree with the person who has shared. Connections has given me more confidence in sharing my thoughts not onlywith classmates, but also with other people. I think Connections has also made me a better writer because now I think I add more detail to my work. Now I believe my imagination, my creativity and my effort all have improved because of Writing and Sharing Connections!

By Dawn Qadir

Categorizing My Connections

Name **Dawn Qadir**

Categories Generated	(12/10/98) Legend of El Dorado	(1/21/99) The Kings Day	(2/4/99) Sir Francis Drake	(2/23/99) The Pirate Queen	(3/4/99) Painter & the Wild Swans	(3/24/99) The Tower of London	(4/15/99) Pizarro's Death	(5/11/99) Thomas Edison	(5/19/99) Tower of London II	(6/99) Princess and the Peacocks	(6/99) Samuel's Choice	(6/99) The Hatmaker's Sign
Famous People				■				■				■
Intertextual Link												
History			■				■					
Media												
Subject											■	
Comparing												
Experience												
Inquisitive	■											
Artist												
Comment		■					■					
Self										■		
Literature Read												

93

higher level thinking skills along with her understanding of text. The progress detected in her writing is confirmed with her description of her thinking about her learning in her final metacognitive piece. Dawn describes her process metacognitively.

During the last part of the year, Dawn continued to connect to more and more learning goals categories in a variety of discourse such as poetry letter writing while balancing point of view and perspective as well (see the learning graph in Appendix C). She developed ways to think critically about literary experiences. She also connected to social studies goals but not to science or math, however.

Chapter 8

Celebrating Diversity

I have learned that when you write, you don't open a notebook and start writing, you think deeper than your top layer of thinking and go beyond! It's like a seed then a root and then finally you bloom into a beautiful flower. When you finish the writing the flower dies, and you start the process all over again.

Raysana

In this chapter I use vignettes to describe diverse students who have benefited from making connections. These students took charge of their learning and went beyond curriculum expectations. Some had to overcome learning disabilities, struggles with English as a second language, lack of motivation, or lack of confidence. But in spite of these difficulties, these children found a way to become confident, successful, motivated learners.

One of my fourth graders stated, "It is amazing that even though we all heard the same story read aloud that we all write and share different connections." This student confirmed what I believe and what research supports (Rosenblatt, 1978): Our background knowledge is diverse. The Writing and Sharing Connections process exposes students' background knowledge so that they make a connection with new information. Another student wrote, "I get ideas from listening to my classmates share their connections, and it helps me to write better connections." Some students have stored knowledge that may be forgotten eventually because it is rarely retrieved. This happens to adults frequently. Writing, sharing, and especially listening to connections from others helps us remember stored knowledge.

Connections Strengthens Special Education

I agree with Taylor and Lytle who believe that "we consistently underestimate the enormous potential of children to participate in the construction of their own learning environments" (1993, p. 3). One day I overheard a conversation one of my fourth graders, who was classified as a special education student, was having with one of his peers, Peter. He said, "Look, there's a flintlock in the corner." And Peter responded, "Yeah, like in the poem by Walt Whitman," to which the special education student added, "Oh yeah, 'Runaway Slave.'"

Some students lack confidence and ability to write connections that reflect their thinking at first. I have found that students who are classified as learning disabled or bilingual can find ways to respond to Writing and Sharing Connections. For these hesitant writers, I usually try to help by doing the following:

1. I encourage them to draw a simple picture of what the literature reminds them of.

2. As their confidence increases, I ask them to write the title of the book on the drawing.

3. Later, I might ask hesitant writers to write one or two words describing what they have drawn.

I find that soon they will become more confident and begin writing connections.

Raysana was classified as a special education student and was reading below grade level when she entered my fourth-grade classroom. She was reluctant to write but loved to hear stories read aloud and participated in discussions. I asked her in the beginning of the year to draw something about a read-aloud story on a sticky note and share it. She complied and drew but refused to share. I finally coaxed her to stand next to me while I described her drawing like this:

Raysana is a little nervous so she has asked me to be her voice this time. How many of you have ever been nervous?

Everyone raised their hands. Then I proceeded to present her illustration as a view about the story that I had not thought of. After we categorized her drawing under the illustration category, the class applauded.

Raysana was timid about sharing her connections in the fall, but by the spring semester she was writing small skits that had point of view and depth. One day, after we read a chapter in *The Story of Thomas Alva Edi-*

son by Margaret Cousins, Raysana asked for a little extra time to complete her connection. When she was finished, she shared it with the class:

> Thomas Edison invented the recording machine but no one really bought it from him. He invented the light bulb too, I guess he had a brain storm. The story of Thomas Edison never ends. People say that he is not a hero and I say, "what?!" But today you will get a better answer than that!

Then Raysana shared a flip book of a drawing of the light bulb. She titled her book *My Story of Thomas Alva Edison*. Because we were studying electricity and had a lesson about the light bulb, she drew a precise step-by-step illustration of the construction of a light bulb. Raysana had taught all of us a new way to respond to text.

Later that year I assigned students to select a recent connection and one written in the fall and compare them. After the selections were made, I conferenced with the children to help them edit their writing. Raysana approached me and said that she thought that I had lost some of her connections during the fall because she could not find any. I asked her to look in her portfolio one more time. Finally she remembered that she had not written many connections early in the year, but had drawn pictures instead. That day she wrote about her Connection process, which she later used as her metacognitive piece:

> Connections make me feel good when Dr. Wooten stands right next to me and I think that's the best part. When Dr. Wooten stands behind me I know that nobody will laugh. My favorite connection was the last one I made with *Who is Carrie?*. I pretended that I was Carrie accepting the "best book award." When I got the award I thanked people like Horace who was the leading man and other important friends. I also quoted my favorite part of the book which was from chapter 13. It stated "I went back to the kitchen and got to work on a heap of potatoes, but my mind wasn't on them. It just kept wandering around, restless like a lost dog that's almost got home but can't find the rest of the way."

Clearly a tremendous leap of learning took place for Raysana. Although her mechanics still needed sharpening, she was generating text that was reflective of her thinking and sharing. (See Raysana's original writing in Figure 21.)

Figure 21 Raysana's Metacognitive Piece

Connections

Raysana

Connections make me feel good when Dr. Wooten stands right next to me and I think that's the best part. When Dr. Wooten stands behind me I know that nobody will laugh. My favorite connection was the last one I made with Who Is Carrie?. I pretended that I was Carrie accepting the" best book award". When I got the award I thanked people like Horace who was the leading man and other important friends. I also quoted my favorite part of the book which was from chapter 13. It stated "I went back to the kitchen and got to work on a heap of potatoes, but my mind wasn't on them. It just kept wandering around, restless like a lost dog that's almost got home but can't find the rest of the way."

Connections Strengthens Bilingual Education

I have witnessed Writing and Sharing Connections advance learning with all types of students, but I was not sure how it was going to work with Hiroe, a new student from Japan who entered my class one year. She knew very little English. We began by going through the steps of the Connections process as best we could, and her connections consisted of her simply copying the title of the book I read aloud to a sticky note. When she came to the front of the room to share, she just said her name and I put her connection under the title category.

The next step was to get Hiroe to say the book title along with her name. I asked another student to help her practice before it was time to share. Students became especially interested in Hiroe's Japanese writing and were supportive throughout the school year. Finally, in December, with the help of her mother as translator, Hiroe wrote her first metacognitive piece:

> I like writing and sharing connections because when I say the title I learn new words. The time line helps me learn more about the past, for instance I learned about Christopher Columbus and how he took four trips to America. I also read an English picture book and a thick Japanese book about Marie Curie and did a report about her. My report also included a time line and a summary about her life. I have written the titles of many books that Dr. Wooten has read to the class and I've drawn lots of picture and conversed with my class about the books that they connected too.

At the end of the school year Hiroe wrote another metacognitive piece with far less help:

> I had a very interesting and challenging year. I learned English well enough to talk to my friends. I was also challenged by new things through the year. In the course of learning English I made a picture dictionary in ESL. I also read books to build up my vocabulary. I sang in chorus and it was a lot of both fun and difficult. I was glad to learn English earlier than my friend in Japan. I was challenged by many things in other classes such as: music, gym, art and computer. I played percussion instruments like conga and rain stick. In gym, I played basketball and volleyball which was very difficult. In art class, I painted using oil paint for the first time. I learned how to type and enjoyed playing games. Above all, the State Project about Georgia because it was the most challenging assignment. I had no trouble drawing picture but writing was hard. I have never done these activities but it was exciting. I am happy that I have learned English and met many new Friends. I want to continue studying English, read many more books and make more friends next year.

Diversity Strengthens All

Writing and Sharing Connections can be an intimidating exercise for some students at first. But the amount that students can learn from one another can be rather amazing. For some students, discovering that they have thoughts in common with their classmates is valuable; and for others, listening to the diversity of thinking about books is helpful.

Writing and Sharing Connections makes students accountable for what they hear and know. Serik, a fourth grader, told me at the beginning of the year that he hated two things: writing and girls. Later in the year, he wrote the following in a metacognitive piece:

> Writing connections makes me listen extra closely to the story and then I think about books, history and my life and come up with one or more connections to write. I enjoy writing them so much that on some of them I write "to be continued...."

The following day, Serik presented me with a follow-up piece. We had just finished reading as a class novel *Who Is Carrie?* (Collier & Collier, 1984), set in 1789 New York City. Carrie was an African American slave who worked for Fraunces, a tavern owner (Fraunces Tavern still stands today in Manhattan). Because we were studying this time period in social studies, this historical fiction text added new life to our curriculum. Serik and his classmates were disappointed to see the story end, so he wrote a continuation to the story at home that night and presented it to me the next day. This sparked a flurry of writing activity as Serik's classmates wrote their own additional chapters to *Who Is Carrie?*. The small steps of the Connections writing process readied everyone for the giant leap of writing a chapter. When students take charge of their learning and it is supported by both peers and the teacher, the quality of work tends to improve greatly.

Another student, who was always wanting to experiment with a new approach to writing, asked one day if he could be the last one to share his connection to *The Tower of London* (Fisher, 1987). As his classmates shared their connections, Scott compiled them into a poem. Everyone was amazed at this idea. He wrote a poem as a connection that also served as his note-taking assignment during the Connections session. Here is Scott's "composite poem connection":

> This is connected to beauty and the beast
> and alcatraze
> the Eiffel tower too.
> This is connected to O'Malley
> and the wild swans are there.
> This is connected to the Great Fire
> and Henry the III was there.
> This is connected to Rapunzel with her hair.
> This is connected to James the I,
> the Tower was there,
> there were graves there too.
> This is connected to the pyramids they were there
> and Edison was also there.
> There were malls there too.
> There were sisters too.
> There was a leaning tower too.
> There was a visiter too.
> This is connected to the zoo and Henry was there.

I close this chapter with an excerpt from Kelly's metacognitive piece:

> I look forward to whenever I get a chance to share and let out what I have written and my ideas. I also enjoy when the time comes to hear other people's thoughts and how they put them into their connections. This way we can learn from each other. Isn't that what our community is all about?

Conclusion

When I started this book it was the last day of a school year. Now, 3 years later, I am still learning and researching Writing and Sharing Connections. How can I improve the effectiveness? How can more of the developmental component in terms of mechanics, content, and writing skills become more visible and manageable for students and educators so that more progress is attainable? Does Writing and Sharing Connections really help prepare students for the next levels of their education? Is it really worthwhile?

In the first few pages of the Introduction you read an incredible note written to me from a student named Andrew. I have remained in contact with several former students over the years and I decided to give Andrew a call. I was taken aback a bit when a much deeper voice answered the phone; Andrew is now in eighth grade. I asked him one simple question: Has Writing and Sharing Connections had any impact on his learning today? Without even a pause he answered quickly:

> Absolutely, because now I have DBQ's [Document Based Questions] and we have to use two or more documents to write a thesis statement. Connections helped because I would have to relate what you had read to us to a "source from my head" and write about it. Sometimes you would even read more than one piece to us too and we would relate to both pieces. Yes, it helped!

Metacognitive thinking at work: Andrew was able to lift the format of learning from one situation and plug it into another.

I have realized that even in this time of emphasis on student achievement accountability that Writing and Sharing Connections has helped prepare students for the latest standardized tests in language arts. The recent standardized test administered in fourth grade in New York state has frustrated a lot of teachers, students, and administrators because of the format and level of difficulty. One part of the test involves the teacher reading aloud a story and students taking notes and then writing about the story. My students have been preparing for this test since the first day of school because they take notes during our read-aloud sessions and

101

while their classmates share their connections aloud. Taking notes, listening, and writing are skills that should be a part of every child's learning portfolio. They are in my classroom.

Many times when sound educational theory is put into practice someone takes the same idea without fully understanding why and what they are implementing and creates a method that needs costly and timely staff development until it is not feasible. Meanwhile, children learn. They listen to stories read aloud, write, listen, talk, think, and more in spite of our methods. Writing and Sharing Connections puts simple learning steps into action for all children. There is not any magic except what the students do with the process. There are support and guidance but no limits. It is manageable for the teacher and it is fun. I know that if you try it you will be amazed at the journey.

When other educators visit my classroom and observe Writing and Sharing Connections already in action, questions always arise. I have answered here some of the most frequently asked questions in hopes that this will help you establish Writing and Sharing Connections in your classroom.

Q. Writing and Sharing Connections looks great for a smaller class size of 18 or 20 students. But I have as many as 35 students in my classroom. What do I do when there's not enough time for all 35 to share their connections?

A. With a large class size you probably have no choice but to have only half of the class share connections aloud in each session. Be sure to maintain an even rotation so that every student is heard in every two sessions. I would suggest that *all* students place their connections on the chart in every session. Then encourage students to go up to the chart and read connections during writers workshop.

Q. What do I do when a student responds to a story in an inappropriate way?

A. I would treat this the same way I would treat inappropriate comments in general. They are not allowed. Usually students who make inappropriate responses need extra attention and coaching in order for you to uncover the insecurities they are hiding.

Q. How do I find good books that connect to what I am teaching?

A. Step one is always to make use of your school librarian. Discuss with him or her the topics you are covering and let him or her lead you to related books. Also, in your search for literature, think a little "out if the box." For example, in studying the *Declaration of Independence*, you can read the declaration. But also think of supporting points of interest surrounding the declaration: the writer, the time period in dress, lifestyle, poetry, art, science, inventions, entertainment, etc. I love to tantalize my students regularly with extra bits of surprising (and entertaining) information. I would look for books that might have information from that period about medical treatment, dining etiquette, crime and punishment, tales of struggle and survival, or struggles between classes and races of people in the time period. I especially enjoy presenting stories of people who have overcome great odds to make achievements. The *Declaration of Independence* had great worldwide implications, so literature about other countries in the time period might be useful. Don't forget to incorporate the art and music of the time.

All this and more should serve as idea starters for you and your librarian. The Internet also has become extremely valuable in searching for excellent Connections literature. I visit www.amazon.com and www.barnesandnoble.com almost weekly to search topics in children's literature. The keyword searches on these Web sites can turn up useful titles. Remember to use Writing and Sharing Connections as an opportunity to break the mold of presenting fact-laden text. Adding a related but unusual presentation can be like a shot of vitamins to your students, shaking up their thinking and waking up their creativity.

Q. What happens if a student refuses to share because he or she is embarrassed or shy?

A. If an inability to write is the cause for timidity, suggest that the student draw a picture reflecting some aspect or symbol of the story. Then encourage the student to stand with you or with a peer and describe what he or she has drawn and how it relates to the story.

Children who are experiencing stage fright might stand with another friend in sharing a connection. Another enticement is to have students present with dramatics or point of view. Some students' self-esteem is so low that expressing themselves is too threatening so becoming another voice, point of view, or object is less intimidating.

Q. What are some steps that a teacher can take to move a student who draws responses to one who writes responses? (This usually refers to a child who is below grade level or non-English speaking.) Or, what do I do when I know a student could be writing deeper connections and gets by with the minimum?

A. Writing connections is perfect for accomplishing this goal because the small sticky note is less intimidating. If this student struggles with print in the connection process then other areas are also lacking print as well. I use much of the writing process approach. Have the student label her drawings and then later conference with the student and have her dictate thinking, allowing you to write the language on a sticky note and then add to the chart. One way to boost a student's self-esteem is to have the student secretly dictate her connection and then have her read it aloud or say it orally and then you write it for the student later and add it to the chart. I still have students bring the sticky note with them with their drawing and put it on the chart. Building self-esteem, supporting students, committing their language to print and allowing them to read it, using a print rich environment for them to refer to, having them keep a reading log that is maintained at home and reviewed by you, and linking the reading, writing, and language process are all things that move children to higher levels of learning.

Q. Why should I add another teaching methodology to my already busy teaching schedule?

A: Writing and Sharing Connections actually will save you time in several ways:

1. Writing and Sharing Connections covers listening, reading, writing, and, depending on the topic of the book, one or more subject areas. (You are also teaching students how to take notes in a manageable way for students and teachers.) So you are addressing several subject areas at one time without planning extra for students with special needs.

2. Students will begin to write and share connections that will cross the boundaries between subject areas. They will begin to integrate the subject areas for you.

3. Students will write connections to previously learned material. This acts as a review of this material. When the entire class hears this type of connection, everyone recieves a mini review lesson.

4. In a short time students will begin to enjoy Writing and Sharing Connections and your discipline problems will tend to be minimized. This helps make learning and teaching fun.

5. Because the connections are permanently posted on a tablet sheet, you will have a progression of documents on hand written by all students and available for an admistrator, parent, student, and/or colleague to probe for assessment or other purposes.

6. If a student is absent or out of the room, it is easy for him or her to make up a connection when returning. I have the returning student read the literature, or have another student read it aloud. The returning student then writes a connection and shares it with the class during a moment of down time.

7. With Writing and Sharing Connections students begin to take control and do the work for you. They construct their learning. I believe that when the students become the teachers, their learning soars.

Q. How do I measure growth?

A. I look at content, mechanics, and creative risks. Creative risks can be reflected within content or mechanics or with the visual aspect of the connection. I look for times in which students begin to think divergently and discover new ways to connect their learning. I am interested in students remembering what they have learned in the past and tying it to new knowledge.

My favorite indicator of growth is when I see a student try something new. A student named Michael was conferring with me during writers workshop one day. He told me that he realized that everything could be connected and a number pattern formed. He wrote in his writer's notebook information gleaned from former connections and the student time line. The special numbers were listed in the margins while all his research and calculations appeared on other parts of the page. He wrote explorers and dates and then subtracted years from one another. He developed a mathematical equation that tied history together in a way I had never thought of. I might add that Michael's least favorite subject was math.

Chelsea's Learning Graph for the First Segment of Connections

Learning Goals/Language Arts	Starry Messenger	The Librarian Who Measured the Earth	Looking for Atlantis	River Ran Wild	Icebergs and Glaciers	Dragon in the Rocks	
1. Comprehends some text.	✔	✔	✔	✔	✔	✔	
2. Fuses new with background knowledge:	✔	✔	✔	✔	✔	✔	
a. Uses intertextual links.						✱	
b. Connects subject areas.					✱		
c. Applies the time line.							
d. Relates experience.		✱	✱	✱		✱	
e. Bridges media.					✱	✔	
3. Supports connection with "why."		✔				✔	
4. Takes notes.	✔	✔	✔	✔	✔	✔	
5. Writes reflectively.		✔			✔	✔	
6. Compares and contrasts.	✔	✔	✔	✔	✔	✔	
7. Takes and defends a position.							
8. Uses divergent thinking.							
9. Asks and answers questions.							
10. Draws conclusions.							
11. Distinguishes fact from opinion.							
12. Recalls content.							
13. Writes connection in form of a letter, etc.							
14. Relates learning to class mate.	✔						
15. Regards various human conditions from perspectives.							
Literature Read *(continued)*							

Learning Goals/Content Specific	Starry Messenger	The Librarian Who Measured the Earth	Looking for Atlantis	River Ran Wild	Icebergs and Glaciers	Dragon in the Rocks				
16. Addresses social studies concepts:										
a. Historical										
b. Geographical										
c. Economic										
d. Civics										
17. Addresses math standards:										
a. Problem solving (S/1)										
b. Communication (S/2)										
c. Reasoning (S/3)										
d. Mathematical connections (S/4)										
e. Estimation (S/5)										
f. Number sense (S/6)										
g. Whole number operation (S/7)										
h. Whole number computation (S/8)										
i. Geometry and spatial sense (S/9)										
j. Measurement (S/10)										
k. Statistics and probability (S/11)										
l. Fractions and decimals (S/12)										
m. Patterns and relationships (S/13)										
18. Addresses science concepts:					✔					
a. Makes observations.					✳					
b. Classifies.										
c. Shows understanding of science.										
d. Shows understanding of earth science.					✳					
e. Shows understanding of life science.										

Note: The social studies and math sections of Chelsea's learning goals graph are not included in this graph because she did not achieve any of the goals listed in those content areas.

Learning Goals/Language Arts	Polar the Titanic Bear	Follow the Dream	Encounter	Sign of the Beaver	Gutenberg	Sir Cumference...	From Hand to Mouth...	Eating the Plates	Rough-Face Girl
1. Comprehends some text.	✔	✔	✔	✔	✔	✔	✔		✔
2. Fuses new with background knowledge:	✔	✔	✔	✔	✔	✔	✔		✔
a. Uses intertextual links.	✱		✱		✱				✱
b. Connects subject areas.	✱				✱				
c. Applies the time line.	✱								
d. Relates experience.	✱	✱	✱	✱					
e. Bridges media.	✱				✱				
3. Supports connection with "why."	✔	✔	✔	✔	✔	✔	✔		✔
4. Takes notes.	✔	✔	✔	✔	✔	✔	✔		✔
5. Writes reflectively.									
6. Compares and contrasts.	✔	✔	✔	✔	✔	✔	✔		✔
7. Takes and defends a position.			✔						✔
8. Uses divergent thinking.									
9. Asks and answers questions.									
10. Draws conclusions.	✔		✔						✔
11. Distinguishes fact from opinion.								ABSENT	
12. Recalls content.	✔		✔						
13. Writes connection in form of a letter, etc.									
14. Relates learning to classmate.									
15. Regards various human conditions from perspectives.			✔						
Literature Read									

(continued)

Learning Goals/Content Specific

	Polar the Titanic Bear	Follow the Dream	Encounter	Sign of the Beaver	Gutenberg	Sir Cumference...	From Hand to Mouth...	Eating the Plates	Rough-Face Girl	
16. Addresses social studies concepts:	✔		✔							
a. Historical	✳									
b. Geographical	✳									
c. Economic										
d. Civics			✳							
17. Addresses math standards:	✳									
a. Problem solving (S/1)	✔									
b. Communication (S/2)	✔									
c. Reasoning (S/3)										
d. Mathematical connections (S/4)										
e. Estimation (S/5)										
f. Number sense (S/6)										
g. Whole number operation (S/7)										
h. Whole number computation (S/8)	✔									
i. Geometry and spatial sense (S/9)										
j. Measurement (S/10)										
k. Statistics and probability (S/11)										
l. Fractions and decimals (S/12)										
m. Patterns and relationships (S/13)	✔									
18. Addresses science concepts:	✔									
a. Makes observations.	✳									
b. Classifies.										
c. Shows understanding of science.									ABSENT		
d. Shows understanding of earth science.										
e. Shows understanding of life science.										
Literature Read										

Learning Goals/Language Arts

	Legend of El Dorado	The King's Day	Sir Francis Drake	The Pirate Queen	Painter & the Wild Swans	The Tower of London	Pizarro's Death	Thomas Edison	Tower of London II	Princess and the Peacocks	Samuel's Choice	The Hatmaker's Sign
1. Comprehends some text.		✔	✔	✔	✔	✔	✔	✔		✔	✔	✔
2. Fuses new with background knowledge:	✔		✔	✔	✔	✔	✔	✔		✔	✔	✔
a. Uses intertextual links.				✶	✶					✶	✶	
b. Connects subject areas.					✶		✶					
c. Applies the time line.			✶	✶			✶	✶				✶
d. Relates experience.							✶	✶		✶		
e. Bridges media.				✶		✶		✶		✶	✶	✶
3. Supports connection with "why."	✔	✔	✔	✔	✔		✔	✔		✔	✔	✔
4. Takes notes.	✔	✔	✔	✔	✔		✔	✔		✔	✔	✔
5. Writes reflectively.				✔	✔		✔	✔		✔		
6. Compares and contrasts.	✔	✔	✔	✔	✔	✔	✔	✔		✔	✔	✔
7. Takes and defends a position.				✔	✔		✔	✔		✔	✔	✔
8. Uses divergent thinking.		✔		✔			✔	✔		✔	✔	✔
9. Asks and answers questions.				✔			✔					
10. Draws conclusions.	✔	✔	✔	✔	✔	✔	✔	✔		✔	✔	
11. Distinguishes fact from opinion.				✔	✔							
12. Recalls content.	✔	✔	✔	✔	✔	✔		✔		✔	✔	✔
13. Writes connection in form of a letter, etc.							✔					
14. Relates learning to classmate.				✔								
15. Regards various human conditions from perspectives.		✔	✔	✔	✔		✔				✔	✔

Literature Read

(continued)

Learning Goals/Content Specific

	Legend of El Dorado	The King's Day	Sir Francis Drake	The Pirate Queen	Painter & the Wild Swans	The Tower of London	Pizarro's Death	Thomas Edison	Tower of London II	Princess and the Peacocks	Samuel's Choice	The Hatmaker's Sign
16. Addresses social studies concepts:	✔	✔	✔	✔			✔	✔				
a. Historical	✱	✱	✱	✱			✱	✱				
b. Geographical			✱				✱					
c. Economic			✱					✱				
d. Civics			✱	✱			✱	✱				
17. Addresses math standards:		✔					✔					
a. Problem solving (S/1)							✱					
b. Communication (S/2)							✱					
c. Reasoning (S/3)												
d. Mathematical connections (S/4)							✱					
e. Estimation (S/5)												
f. Number sense (S/6)		✱										
g. Whole number operation (S/7)							✱					
h. Whole number computation (S/8)												
i. Geometry and spatial sense (S/9)												
j. Measurement (S/10)												
k. Statistics and probability (S/11)												
l. Fractions and decimals (S/12)												
m. Patterns and relationships (S/13)												
18. Addresses science concepts:		✔			✔	✔		✔				
a. Makes observations.		✱			✱	✱		✱				
b. Classifies.												
c. Shows understanding of science.												
d. Shows understanding of earth science.		✱										
e. Shows understanding of life science.												
Literature Read												

Brian's Learning Graph for the First Segment of Connections

Learning Goals/Language Arts	Starry Messenger	The Librarian Who Measured the Earth	Looking for Atlantis	River Ran Wild	Icebergs and Glaciers	Dragon in the Rocks	
1. Comprehends some text.	✔	✔	✔	✔	✔	✔	
2. Fuses new with background knowledge:	✔	✔	✔	✔	✔	✔	
a. Uses intertextual links.			✱		✱	✱	
b. Connects subject areas.							
c. Applies the time line.							
d. Relates experience.	✱	✱		✱			
e. Bridges media.							
3. Supports connection with "why."		✔	✔	✔	✔	✔	
4. Takes notes.	✔	✔	✔	✔	✔	✔	
5. Writes reflectively.							
6. Compares and contrasts.	✔	✔	✔	✔	✔	✔	
7. Takes and defends a position.							
8. Uses divergent thinking.							
9. Asks and answers questions.							
10. Draws conclusions.							
11. Distinguishes fact from opinion.							
12. Recalls content.							
13. Writes connection in form of a letter, etc.							
14. Relates learning to class mate.							
15. Regards various human conditions from perspectives.							
Literature Read							

Note: The content area sections of Brian's learning graph are not included in this graph because he did not achieve any of the content-specific goals.

Learning Goals/Language Arts	Polar the Titanic Bear	Follow the Dream	Encounter	Sign of the Beaver	Gutenberg	Sir Cumference...	From Hand to Mouth...	Eating the Plates	Rough-Face Girl	
1. Comprehends some text.	✔	✔	✔	✔	✔	✔	✔	✔	✔	
2. Fuses new with background knowledge:	✔	✔	✔	✔	✔	✔	✔	✔	✔	
a. Uses intertextual links.		✳	✳				✳		✳	
b. Connects subject areas.					✳	✳				
c. Applies the time line.					✳					
d. Relates experience.	✳	✳	✳	✳	✳		✳	✳	✳	
e. Bridges media.										
3. Supports connection with "why."	✔	✔	✔	✔	✔	✔	✔	✔	✔	
4. Takes notes.	✔	✔	✔	✔	✔	✔	✔	✔	✔	
5. Writes reflectively.					✔					
6. Compares and contrasts.	✔	✔	✔	✔	✔	✔	✔	✔	✔	
7. Takes and defends a position.										
8. Uses divergent thinking.					✔					
9. Asks and answers questions.										
10. Draws conclusions.					✔					
11. Distinguishes fact from opinion.										
12. Recalls content.					✔					
13. Writes connection in form of a letter, etc.										
14. Relates learning to classmate.										
15. Regards various human conditions from perspectives.										
Literature Read										

(continued)

113

Learning Goals/Content Specific

	Polar the Titanic Bear	Follow the Dream	Encounter	Sign of the Beaver	Gutenberg	Sir Cumference...	From Hand to Mouth...	Eating the Plates	Rough-Face Girl
16. Addresses social studies concepts:					✔				
a. Historical					✳				
b. Geographical									
c. Economic									
d. Civics									
17. Addresses math standards:					✔				
a. Problem solving (S/1)					✳				
b. Communication (S/2)					✳				
c. Reasoning (S/3)									
d. Mathematical connections (S/4)					✳				
e. Estimation (S/5)									
f. Number sense (S/6)									
g. Whole number operation (S/7)									
h. Whole number computation (S/8)					✳				
i. Geometry and spatial sense (S/9)									
j. Measurement (S/10)									
k. Statistics and probability (S/11)									
l. Fractions and decimals (S/12)									
m. Patterns and relationships (S/13)									
18. Addresses science concepts:					✔				
a. Makes observations.					✳				
b. Classifies.									
c. Shows understanding of science.									
d. Shows understanding of earth science.									
e. Shows understanding of life science.									
Literature Read									

Learning Goals/Language Arts

Learning Goals/Language Arts	Legend of El Dorado	The King's Day	Sir Francis Drake	The Pirate Queen	Painter & the Wild Swans	The Tower of London	Pizarro's Death	Thomas Edison	Tower of London II	Princess and the Peacocks	Samuel's Choice	The Hatmaker's Sign
1. Comprehends some text.	✔	✔	✔	✔	✔	✔		✔		✔	✔	✔
2. Fuses new with background knowledge:	✔	✔	✔	✔	✔	✔		✔		✔	✔	✔
a. Uses intertextual links.	✳				✳					✳	✳	✳
b. Connects subject areas.	✳					✳						
c. Applies the time line.	✳											
d. Relates experience.	✳		✳		✳			✳		✳	✳	✳
e. Bridges media.								✳				
3. Supports connection with "why."	✔	✔	✔	✔	✔	✔				✔	✔	✔
4. Takes notes.	✔	✔	✔	✔	✔	✔				✔	✔	✔
5. Writes reflectively.	✔				✔			✔				
6. Compares and contrasts.	✔	✔	✔	✔	✔	✔		✔		✔	✔	✔
7. Takes and defends a position.				✔		✔		✔				
8. Uses divergent thinking.	✔			✔				✔				
9. Asks and answers questions.											✔	✔
10. Draws conclusions.	✔							✔			✔	✔
11. Distinguishes fact from opinion.				✔								
12. Recalls content.	✔	✔		✔	✔	✔				✔	✔	✔
13. Writes connection in form of a letter, etc.				✔	✔			✔				✔
14. Relates learning to class mate.	✔							✔		✔		
15. Regards various human conditions from perspectives.	✔			✔		✔		✔				✔
Literature Read												

(continued)

Brian's Learning Graph for the Third Segment of Connections (continued)

Learning Goals/Content Specific	Legend of El Dorado	The King's Day	Sir Francis Drake	The Pirate Queen	Painter & the Wild Swans	The Tower of London	Pizarro's Death	Thomas Edison	Tower of London II	Princess and the Peacocks	Samuel's Choice	The Hatmaker's Sign
16. Addresses social studies concepts:	✔			✔							✔	✔
a. Historical	✳			✳							✳	
b. Geographical	✳			✳								
c. Economic	✳			✳								✳
d. Civics	✳			✳								
17. Addresses math standards:	✔											
a. Problem solving (S/1)												
b. Communication (S/2)	✳											
c. Reasoning (S/3)												
d. Mathematical connections (S/4)	✳											
e. Estimation (S/5)												
f. Number sense (S/6)												
g. Whole number operation (S/7)												
h. Whole number computation (S/8)	✳											
i. Geometry and spatial sense (S/9)												
j. Measurement (S/10)												
k. Statistics and probability (S/11)												
l. Fractions and decimals (S/12)												
m. Patterns and relationships (S/13)	✳											
18. Addresses science concepts:	✔			✔	✔							
a. Makes observations.	✳			✳	✳							
b. Classifies.												
c. Shows understanding of science.				✳								
d. Shows understanding of earth science.												
e. Shows understanding of life science.												
Literature Read												

Dawn's Learning Graph for the First Segment of Connections

Learning Goals/Language Arts	Starry Messenger	The Librarian Who Measured the Earth	Looking for Atlantis	River Ran Wild	Icebergs and Glaciers	Dragon in the Rocks	
1. Comprehends some text.	✔	✔	✔	✔	✔	✔	
2. Fuses new with background knowledge:	✔	✔	✔	✔	✔	✔	
a. Uses intertextual links.			✱				
b. Connects subject areas.					✱		
c. Applies the time line.							
d. Relates experience.							
e. Bridges media.	✱		✱				
3. Supports connection with "why."	✔	✔	✔	✔	✔	✔	
4. Takes notes.	✔	✔	✔	✔	✔	✔	
5. Writes reflectively.							
6. Compares and contrasts.	✔	✔	✔	✔	✔	✔	
7. Takes and defends a position.							
8. Uses divergent thinking.							
9. Asks and answers questions.							
10. Draws conclusions.		✔					
11. Distinguishes fact from opinion.							
12. Recalls content.					✔		
13. Writes connection in form of a letter, etc.							
14. Relates learning to classmate.							
15. Regards various human conditions from perspectives.		✔					
Literature Read	Starry Messenger	The Librarian Who Measured the Earth	Looking for Atlantis	River Ran Wild	Icebergs and Glaciers	Dragon in the Rocks	

Learning Goals/Content Specific	Starry Messenger	The Librarian Who Measured the Earth	Looking for Atlantis	River Ran Wild	Icebergs and Glaciers	Dragon in the Rocks				
16. Addresses social studies concepts:										
a. Historical										
b. Geographical										
c. Economic										
d. Civics										
17. Addresses math standards:										
a. Problem solving (S/1)										
b. Communication (S/2)										
c. Reasoning (S/3)										
d. Mathematical connections (S/4)										
e. Estimation (S/5)										
f. Number sense (S/6)										
g. Whole number operation (S/7)										
h. Whole number computation (S/8)										
i. Geometry and spatial sense (S/9)										
j. Measurement (S/10)										
k. Statistics and probability (S/11)										
l. Fractions and decimals (S/12)										
m. Patterns and relationships (S/13)										
18. Addresses science concepts:					✳					
a. Makes observations.					✔					
b. Classifies.										
c. Shows understanding of science.										
d. Shows understanding of earth science.					✔					
e. Shows understanding of life science.										
Literature Read										

Note: The social studies and math sections of Dawn's learning goals graph are not included in this graph because she did not achieve any of the goals listed in those content areas.

Dawn's Learning Graph for the Second Segment of Connections

Learning Goals/Language Arts	Polar the Titanic Bear	Follow the Dream	Encounter	Sign of the Beaver	Gutenberg	Sir Cumference...	From Hand to Mouth...	Eating the Plates	Rough-Face Girl	
1. Comprehends some text.	✔	✔	✔	✔	✔		✔	✔	✔	
2. Fuses new with background knowledge:	✔	✔	✔	✔	✔		✔	✔	✔	
a. Uses intertextual links.			✱							
b. Connects subject areas.										
c. Applies the time line.										
d. Relates experience.	✱	✱	✱	✱	✱		✱	✱	✱	
e. Bridges media.			✱							
3. Supports connection with "why."	✔	✔	✔	✔	✔		✔	✔	✔	
4. Takes notes.	✔	✔	✔	✔	✔		✔	✔	✔	
5. Writes reflectively.		✔								
6. Compares and contrasts.	✔		✔	✔			✔	✔	✔	
7. Takes and defends a position.										
8. Uses divergent thinking.		✔								
9. Asks and answers questions.										
10. Draws conclusions.		✔								
11. Distinguishes fact from opinion.										
12. Recalls content.		✔								
13. Writes connection in form of a letter, etc.										
14. Relates learning to classmate.										
15. Regards various human conditions from perspectives.		✔	✔		✔		✔	✔	✔	

Literature Read

(continued)

Learning Goals/Content Specific

	Polar the Titanic Bear	Follow the Dream	Encounter	Sign of the Beaver	Gutenberg	Sir Cumference...	From Hand to Mouth...	Eating the Plates	Rough-Face Girl
16. Addresses social studies concepts:			✔						
a. Historical			✳						
b. Geographical									
c. Economic									
d. Civics									
17. Addresses math standards:									
a. Problem solving (S/1)									
b. Communication (S/2)									
c. Reasoning (S/3)									
d. Mathematical connections (S/4)									
e. Estimation (S/5)									
f. Number sense (S/6)									
g. Whole number operation (S/7)									
h. Whole number computation (S/8)									
i. Geometry and spatial sense (S/9)									
j. Measurement (S/10)									
k. Statistics and probability (S/11)									
l. Fractions and decimals (S/12)									
m. Patterns and relationships (S/13)									
18. Addresses science concepts:									
a. Makes observations.									
b. Classifies.									
c. Shows understanding of science.									
d. Shows understanding of earth science.									
e. Shows understanding of life science.									
Literature Read									

Note: The math and science sections of Dawn's learning goals graph are not included in this graph because she did not achieve any of the goals listed in those content areas.

Learning Goals/Language Arts

Learning Goals/Language Arts	Legend of El Dorado	The King's Day	Sir Francis Drake	The Pirate Queen	Painter & the Wild Swans	The Tower of London	Pizarro's Death	Thomas Edison	Tower of London II	Princess and the Peacocks	Samuel's Choice	The Hatmaker's Sign
1. Comprehends some text.	✔	✔	✔	✔		✔	✔	✔			✔	✔
2. Fuses new with background knowledge:	✔		✔	✔		✔	✔	✔			✔	✔
a. Uses intertextual links.			✳			✳	✳	✳			✳	✳
b. Connects subject areas.						✳	✳					✳
c. Applies the time line.						✳	✳					✳
d. Relates experience.	✳		✳	✳		✳						✳
e. Bridges media.						✳	✳				✳	✔
3. Supports connection with "why."	✔	✔	✔	✔		✔	✔	✔			✔	✔
4. Takes notes.	✔	✔	✔	✔		✔	✔	✔			✔	
5. Writes reflectively.			✔								✔	✔
6. Compares and contrasts.	✔	✔	✔	✔			✔	✔			✔	✔
7. Takes and defends a position.			✔			✔	✔				✔	✔
8. Uses divergent thinking.			✔			✔	✔				✔	
9. Asks and answers questions.												
10. Draws conclusions.		✔	✔	✔		✔	✔	✔				✔
11. Distinguishes fact from opinion.					(ABSENT)						✔	
12. Recalls content.			✔		(ABSENT)	✔	✔	✔			✔	✔
13. Writes connection in form of a letter, etc.		✔	✔		(ABSENT)		✔				✔	
14. Relates learning to classmate.												✔
15. Regards various human conditions from perspectives.			✔	✔			✔					✔

Literature Read

(continued)

Dawn's Learning Graph for the Third Segment of Connections (continued)

Learning Goals/Content Specific	Legend of El Dorado	The King's Day	Sir Francis Drake	The Pirate Queen	Painter & the Wild Swans	The Tower of London	Pizarro's Death	Thomas Edison	Tower of London II	Princess and the Peacocks	Samuel's Choice	The Hatmaker's Sign
16. Addresses social studies concepts:			✔	✔		✔	✔				✔	✔
a. Historical			✳			✳	✳				✳	✳
b. Geographical				✳			✳				✳	✳
c. Economic				✳			✳				✳	✳
d. Civics											✳	✳
17. Addresses math standards:												
a. Problem solving (S/1)												
b. Communication (S/2)												
c. Reasoning (S/3)												
d. Mathematical connections (S/4)												
e. Estimation (S/5)												
f. Number sense (S/6)												
g. Whole number operation (S/7)												
h. Whole number computation (S/8)												
i. Geometry and spatial sense (S/9)												
j. Measurement (S/10)												
k. Statistics and probability (S/11)												
l. Fractions and decimals (S/12)												
m. Patterns and relationships (S/13)												
18. Addresses science concepts:												
a. Makes observations.												
b. Classifies.												
c. Shows understanding of science.												
d. Shows understanding of earth science.												
e. Shows understanding of life science.												
Literature Read	Legend of El Dorado	The King's Day	Sir Francis Drake	The Pirate Queen	Painter & the Wild Swans	The Tower of London	Pizarro's Death	Thomas Edison	Tower of London II	Princess and the Peacocks	Samuel's Choice	The Hatmaker's Sign

Note: The math and science sections of Dawn's learning goals graph are not included in this graph because she did not achieve any of the goals listed in those content areas.

References

Anderson, R.C., Hiebert, E.H., Scott, J.A., & Wilkerson, I.A.G. (1985). *Becoming a nation of readers: The report of the Commission on Reading*. Washington, DC: U.S. Department of Education.

Andrade, H. (2000). Using rubrics to promote thinking and learning. *Educational Leadership, 57*(5), 13–18.

Bird, L.B., & Goodman, Y. (1994). *The whole language catalog: Forms for authentic assessment*. Columbus, OH: SRA/McGraw-Hill.

Britton, J.N. (1970). *Language and learning*. London: Penguin.

Britton, J.N., Burgess, T., Martin, N., McLeod, A., & Rosen, H. (1975). *Development of writing abilities*. New York: Macmillan.

Brooks, M., & Brooks, J. (1999). The courage to be constructivist. *Educational Leadership, 57*(3), 18–24.

Bruce, B.C. (1983). *Action! Suspense! Culture! Insight! Reading stories in the classroom*. Arlington, VA. (ERIC Document Reproduction Service No. ED 237 929)

Bruner, J.S. (1966). *Toward a theory of instruction*. Cambridge, MA: The Belknap Press of Harvard University.

Buzan, T., & Buzan, B. (1996). *The mind map book: How to use radiant thinking to maximize your brain's untapped potential*. New York: Penguin.

Calkins, L.M. (1994). *The art of teaching writing*. Portsmouth, NH: Heinemann.

Cullinan, B.E., & Galda, L. (1998). *Literature and the child* (4th ed.). San Diego, CA: Harcourt Brace.

Feitelson, D. (1988). *Facts and fads in beginning reading: A cross-language perspective*. Norwood, NJ: Ablex.

Fox, M. (1997). Toward a personal theory of whole language: A teacher-researcher-writer reflects. In J. Turbill & B. Cambourne (Eds.), *The changing face of whole language* (pp. 33–42). Newark, DE: International Reading Association.

Galda, L., Cullinan, B.E., & Strickland, D.S. (1997). *Language, literacy and the child*. San Diego, CA: Harcourt Brace.

Galda, L., & West, J. (1995). Exploring literature through drama. In N.L. Roser & M.G. Martinez (Eds.), *Book talk and beyond: Children and teachers respond to literature* (pp. 183–190). Newark, DE: International Reading Association.

Genishi, C., McCarrier, A., & Nussbaum, N. (1988). Research currents: Dialogue as a context for teaching and learning. *Language Arts, 65*, 182–191.

Graves, D.H. (1983). *Writing: Teachers and children at work*. Portsmouth, NH: Heinemann.

Graves, D.H. (1991). *Build a literate classroom*. Portsmouth, NH: Heinemann.

Hancock, J. (Ed.). (1999). *The explicit teaching of reading*. Newark, DE: International Reading Association.

Hennings, D.G. (1992). *Beyond the read aloud: Learning to read through listening to and reflecting on literature* (25th Anniversary Educational Foundation). Bloomington, IN: The Phi Delta Kappa Educational Foundation.

Iverson, S. (1996). A metacognitive strategy approach to teaching reading: How appropriate and assisted instruction can help all children become readers. *Balanced Reading Instruction, 3*(1), 12–18.

Johns, J.L., & Lenski, S.D. (1997). *Improving reading: A handbook of strategies* (2nd ed.). Dubuque, IA: Kendall/Hunt.

Johnston, P.H. (1997). *Knowing literacy: Constructive literacy assessment*. York, ME: Stenhouse.

Karolides, N. (1999). Theory and practice: An interview with Louise M. Rosenblatt. *Language Arts, 77*(2), 164.

Kendall, J.S., & Marzano, R.J. (1997). *Content knowledge: A compendium of standards and benchmarks for K–12 education* (2nd ed.). Alexandria, VA: Association for Supervision and Curriculum Development.

Krynock, K., & Robb, L. (1999). Problem solved: How to coach cognition. *Educational Leadership, 57*(3), 29–32.

Langer, J.A. (1992). *Literature instruction: A focus on student response*. Urbana, IL: National Council of Teachers of English.

Martin, N. (1987). *Writing across the curriculum*. Upper Montclair, NJ: Boynton/Cook-Heinemann.

Mayher, J.S., Lester, N.B., & Pradl, G.M. (1983). *Learning to write/writing to learn*. Upper Montclair, NJ: Boynton/Cook-Heinemann.

McCormick, S. (1977). Should you read aloud to your children? *Language Arts, 54*(2), 139–143, 163.

McMahon, S.I., & Raphael, T.E. (1997). *The book club connection: Literacy learning and classroom talk*. New York: Teachers College Press; Newark, DE: International Reading Association.

Medway, P. (1976). Lecture notes. In N. Martin, P. D'Arcy, B. Newton, & R. Parker (Eds.), *Writing and learning across the curriculum* (pp. 145–146). Portsmouth, NH: Boynton/Cook.

Michener, D.M. (1988). Test your reading aloud IQ. *The Reading Teacher, 42*(2), 118–122.

Morrow, L.M. (1988). Effects of structural guidance in story retelling on children's dictation of original stories. *Journal of Reading Behaviors, 18*(2), 135–152.

National Council of Teachers of Mathematics. (1992). *Curriculum and evaluation standards for school mathematics*. Reston, VA: Author.

Perkins, D. (1999). The many faces of constructivism. *Educational Leadership, 57*(3), 6–11.

Peterson, R.L. (1992). *Life in a crowded place: Making a learning community*. Portsmouth, NH: Heinemann.

Power, B.M. (1998). *Taking note: Improving your observational note taking*. York, ME: Stenhouse.

Raphael, T.E., Pardo, L.S., Highfield, K., & McMahon, S.I. (1997). *Book Club: A literature-based curriculum*. Littleton, MA: Small Planet Communications.

Rosenblatt, L.M. (1976). *Literature as exploration* (3rd ed.). New York: Modern Language Association. (Original work published 1938)

Rosenblatt, L.M. (1978). *The reader, the text and the poem: The transactional theory of the literary work.* Carbondale, IL: Southern Illinois University Press.

Shaughnessy, M.P. (1977). *Errors & expectations: A guide for the teacher of basic writing.* New York: Oxford University Press.

Shuy, R.W. (1987). Research currents: Dialogue as the heart of learning. *Language Arts, 64,* 890–897.

Steffensen, M.S., Joag-Dev, C., & Anderson, R.C. (1979). A cross-cultural perspective on reading comprehension. *Reading Research Quarterly, 15*(1), 10–29.

Taylor, D., & Lytle, S.L. (1993). *From the child's point of view.* Portsmouth, NH: Heinemann.

Taylor, D., Coughlin, D., & Marasco, J. (1997). *Teaching and advocacy.* York, ME: Stenhouse.

Thelen, J.N. (1986). Vocabulary instruction and meaningful learning. *Journal of Reading, 29,* 603–609.

Vacca, R., & Linek, W. (1992). Writing to learn. In J.W. Irwin & M.A. Doyle (Eds.), *Reading/writing connections: Learning from research* (pp. 145–159). Newark, DE: International Reading Association.

Vygotsky, L.S. (1978). *Mind in society. The development of higher psychological processes.* (M. Cole, V. John-Steiner, S. Scribner, & E. Souberman, Eds. and Trans.). Cambridge, MA: Harvard University Press. (Original work published 1934)

Weaver, C. (1994). *Reading process and practice: From socio-psycholinguistics to whole language* (2nd ed.). Portsmouth, NH: Heinemann.

Wells, G. (1986). *The meaning makers: Children learning language and using language to learn.* Portsmouth, NH: Heinemann.

Wilkinson, L. (1999). An introduction to the explicit teaching of reading. In J. Hancock (Ed.), *The explicit teaching of reading* (pp. 1–10). Newark DE: International Reading Association.

Children's Literature References

Aliki. (1989). *The King's day: Louis XIV of France.* New York: Harper Trophy.

Bathroom Readers' Institute. (1997). *Uncle John's giant 10th anniversary bathroom reader.* Ashland, OR: Bathroom Readers' Press.

Berleth, R.J. (1990). In J. Mathews (Ed.), *Samuel's choice.* New York: Whitman.

Burnett, F.H. (1963). *The Secret Garden.* New York: Viking.

Cherry, L. (1992). *River ran wild: An environmental history.* New York: Dutton.

Clement, C. (1993). *Painter and the wild swans.* New York: Puffin.

Collier, J.L., & Collier, C. (1984). *Who is Carrie?* New York: Yearling.

Cousins, M. (1981). *The story of Thomas Alva Edison.* New York: Random House.

Day, M. (1995). *Dragon in the rocks: A story based on the childhood of the early paleontologist Mary Anning.* Toronto, ON: Greey de Pencier Books.

Fisher, E. (1987). *The tower of London.* New York: Macmillan.

Fisher, L.E. (1993). *Gutenberg.* New York: Simon & Schuster.

Fleming, C. (1998). *The hatmaker's sign: A story by Benjamin Franklin*. New York: Orchard Books.

Frost, R. (1969). The road not taken. In E.C. Lathem (Ed.), *The poetry of Robert Frost*. New York: Henry Holt.

Gerrard, R. (1988). *Sir Francis Drake: His daring deeds*. New York: Farrar, Straus & Giroux.

Giblin, J.C. (1987). *From hand to mouth, or, how we invented knives, forks, spoons, and chopsticks and the table manners to go with them*. New York: Harper.

Gormley, B. (1996). *Back to the day Lincoln was shot*! New York: Scholastic.

Hakim, J. (1999). *First Americans*. New York: Oxford University Press.

Kenda, M., & Williams, P.S. (1995). *Math wizardry for kids*. New York: Barron's.

Lasky, K. (1994). *The librarian who measured the earth*. New York: Little, Brown.

Martin, R. (1992). *Rough-face girl*. New York: Putnam

McCully, E.A. (1995). *The Pirate Queen*. New York: Putman.

Melville, H. (1981). *Moby Dick*. New York: Bantam Classic and Love Sweet.

Merrill, L., & Ridley, S. (1993). *The princess and the peacocks or, the story of the room*. New York: Hyperion.

Neuschwander, C. (1997). *Sir Cumference and the first round table: A math adventure*. Watertown, MA: Charlesbridge.

Penner, L.R. (1991). *Eating the plates: A Pilgrim book of food and manners*. New York: Aladdin Paperbacks.

Poe, E.A. (1991). El Dorado. In M. Rosen (Ed.), *The Kingfisher book of children's poetry*. London: Kingfisher.

Prevert, J. (1991). The Eclipse. In M. Rosen (Ed.), *The Kingfisher book of children's poetry*. London: Kingfisher.

Sandburg, C. (1955). Arithmetic. In H. Plotz (Ed.), *From imagination's other place: Poems of science and mathematics* (p. 78). New York: Harper & Row.

San Souci, R.D. (1994). *Sootface: An Ojibwa Cinderella story*. New York: Four Winds/Macmillan.

Simon, S. (1987). *Icebergs and glaciers*. New York: Morrow.

Sis, P. (1991). *Follow the dream: The story of Christopher Columbus*. New York: Knopf.

Sis, P. (1996). *Starry messenger: A book depicting the life of a famous scientist, mathematician, astronomer, philosopher, physicist Galileo Galilei*. New York: Farrar, Straus & Giroux.

Speare, E.G. (1983). *The sign of the beaver*. New York: Bantam Doubleday Dell.

Spedden, D.C.S. (1994). *Polar the titanic bear*. Boston: Little, Brown.

Thompson, C.E. (1993). *Looking for Atlantis*. New York: Knopf.

Turner, A.W. (1987). *Nettie's trip south*. New York: Macmillan.

Van Laan, N. (1991). *The legend of El Dorado: A Latin American tale*. New York: Knopf.

Whitman, W. (1991). O Captain! My Captain! In M. Rosen (Ed.), *The Kingfisher book of children's poetry*. London: Kingfisher.

Yolen, J. (1992). *Encounter*. San Diego, CA: Harcourt Brace.

Yolen, J. (1995). *The ballad of the pirate queens*. San Diego, CA: Harcourt Brace.

Index